中美版权争议的修辞学研究

董秋敏 著

Copyright Approaches of the United States and China:
A Rhetorical Perspective

河南大学出版社
HENAN UNIVERSITY PRESS
·郑州·

图书在版编目（CIP）数据

中美版权争议的修辞学研究：英文/董秋敏著. —郑州：河南大学出版社，2013.5

ISBN 978-7-5649-1219-2

Ⅰ.①中… Ⅱ.①董… Ⅲ.①比较修辞学－研究－英文②版权－对比研究－中国、美国－英文 Ⅳ.①H05②D923.414③D971.23

中国版本图书馆CIP数据核字（2013）第100537号

责任编辑 卢志宇
责任校对 宋达华
封面设计 马 龙

出版发行	河南大学出版社				
	地址：郑州市郑东新区商务外环中华大厦2401号				
	邮编：450046				
	电话：0371-86059701（营销部）				
	网址：www.hupress.com				
排 版	理光文印设计中心				
印 刷	郑州市今日文教印制有限公司				
版 次	2017年10月第1版		印 次	2017年10月第1次印刷	
开 本	650mm×960mm 1/16		印 张	13.25	
字 数	178千字		定 价	28.00元	

（本书如有印装质量问题请与河南大学出版社营销部联系调换）

前　言

　　中美知识产权/版权纠纷从上世纪 90 年代初中国颁布《中华人民共和国著作权法》、《中华人民共和国著作权法实施条例》和加入《伯尔尼公约》以来从来没有停止过。在过去的二十多年里，中国几乎年年被美国"特别 301 条款"列为对知识产权没有提供充分和有效保护的"重点国家"或"重点观察国家"。因此，知识产权保护问题就成为中美贸易的最大障碍之一。美国对中国知识产权保护的期望和中国对知识产权保护的现状之间的差距不仅成为两国政府贸易谈判的重点，也成为学界关注中美关系的热点。到目前为止，西方学者，特别是美国学者对中美知识产权纠纷的研究主要集中在政治、法律和经济领域，他们的结论是：两个原因导致了知识产权在中国得不到有效保护。其一，中国政府一切以维护政治统治为中心，忽视对知识产权的保护；其二，中国对知识产权的侵权行为缺乏有效的监督，打击力度不够，执法人员不合格和执法不专业，司法不独立。经济学家们认为，有效的知识产权保护将吸引更多的外来投资，从而促进中国的经济发展。因此，他们建议中国政府加强对知识产权的保护，加大对违法行为的打击力度。笔者认为，一个国家、一种文化对包括知识产权在内的法律的认识和态度是个复杂的问题，它们不仅受政治倾向和法制意识的影响，而且，修辞传统和文化背景的差异以及知识产权全球化运动这些因素都应该考虑在内。因此，本书以修辞学的视角，运用比较/对比修辞、跨文化交流和意识形态批评的方法，分析了中西古典修辞学著作、中美现代法律和政令以及中美版权协议的3套共12个文本资料，用以回答两个问题：*中美两国的修辞和文化传统以及版权国际化怎样影响两国对版权保护的认识的法律实施？这种影响对中美专业交流有何意义？*

选择修辞批评探讨中美版权争议是基于美国修辞学家乔治·肯尼迪的修辞实践的普遍性和文化特殊性观点以及肯尼斯·伯克的话语动机理论。伯克认为，词语，即语言信号创造行为的取向和态度，而人作为"使用符号的动物，用话语形成态度或导致他人采取行动"。肯尼迪认为，修辞实践在各种文化中普遍存在，但是每一种文化的修辞实践具有其独特的文化特点。我们可以这样认为，每种文化的修辞传统以话语的形式反映出来并影响人们对事物的态度和行为。因此，分析中美对版权问题的不同认识和态度可以通过研究对两国文化的思维方式以及行为模式的形成产生巨大影响的著作或文本。两国对版权问题之所以存在争端，部分原因也正是因为它们之间的认识存在差异，需要互相了解和理解，"研究误解和弥补方法"（理查兹）和了解修辞在不同交际环境中的作用（肯尼迪）也正是修辞学研究的意义所在。

本书共由六个章组成。第一章引言部分首先引入本研究的出发点、背景、目的、研究的问题，以及本书的组成部分。同时，本章还回顾和综述了中美版权纠纷领域已有的研究文献，即美国学界从中国政治、版权立法和执法以及经济三个领域对纠纷展开的研究以及这些研究的不足之处。引言还描述了修辞研究的理论框架，也就是：（1）柏拉图、亚里士多德、西塞罗相对于孔子、孟子和老子的道德观，他们分别代表古希腊-罗马和中国的修辞传统；(2)

中美不同的文化价值取向，即普遍主义、个人主义对应特殊主义和集体主义以及权利差距；（3）版权全球化运动背景下的中美版权保护争端反映了中美意识形态差异。第一章的最后对修辞的不同定义提供了解释，同时还简要叙述了修辞和本研究的关系。

第二章着重介绍研究方法。首先作者描述了比较和对比中美修辞传统和文化差异的方法，然后把中美版权纠纷放置于对两国版权保护态度和有关法律产生巨大影响的版权全球化的背景之下。该章解释了使用三种研究方法的理由，这三种方法是：以集群分析比较和对比修辞传统、用文化维度揭示中美价值差异和以意识形态批评讨论版权国际化。同时，该章还描述了本书所要讨论的修辞文本和文本的重要章节，分析了为什么本研究所采用的修辞批评方法优于质性和量性分析。最后，描述了所选文本和研究课题的密切关系和本人作为研究者所扮演的角色，以及研究结果的可靠性和有效性。

第三章至第五章是本书的主体。第三章为文本分析的第一部分，聚焦于中西（美）修辞传统对两种文化中人们的道德观念和对法律（版权）意识的影响。集群分析的重点为古希腊-罗马和中国的六部古典修辞著作中的中西道德观念以及相关理念，这些著作是《普罗塔哥拉》、《修辞学》、《论演说家》、《论语》、《孟子》和《道德经》。该章讨论的问题是：所选修辞文本的作者怎样通过道德观以及相关理念劝告人们恪守与法律有关的信念和价值观？

第四章比较和对比三种文化维度对中美法律（版权）观念的影响，同时也论述了修辞传统和不同文化环境下人们的信念、思想和价值观形成的联系。该章所分析的文本是《独立宣言》、《美国宪法》、《中华人民共和国宪法》和《邓小平南方讲话》。该章所要回答的问题是：什么文化信念、思想和价值观对中美法律（版权）实践产生了持续影响？

第五章中作者以中美在20世纪90年代初的版权纠纷为例，用意识形态批评的方法探讨版权全球化背景下中美关于版权的争议。该章首先介绍了中美版权争议的历史背景，即版权发展的两个阶段，代表文本为《伯尔尼公约》和《与贸易有关的知识产权协议》，然后分析了《中美两国政府关于保护知识产权的谅解备忘录》和《中美知识产权保护协议》。作者认为，双方的矛盾中有操纵、恐吓、妥协、服从的特点，这些特点正是古典马克思主义批评和葛兰西文化霸权主义批评的关注重点，这种意识形态的冲突也反映了两种文化对版权保护的认识。作者通过分析回答的问题是：透过中美版权纠纷，版权全球化怎样对两国版权保护意识产生影响？

第六章对全书作出总结，其中包括该研究的理论依据，即比较修辞、跨文化修辞/交流和马克思主义/意识形态批评。这些理论认为人类使用语言阐释周围的世界并创造知识，而这些阐释和知识反过来影响人类的思维、思想和价值观。也就是说，人类对社会的认识属于社会建构，他们的所见、所闻、所学反映在他们的行为和态度上。然后，该章总结了研究的结果和意义，并对同一领域的未来研究者和中美法律/版权保护政策决策者提出了自己的见解。

从完成中美版权争议的修辞学研究到本书出版经过了一年多的时间，中美两国在各个领域的交流合作仍然以上升的趋势发展着，笔者真诚地希望中美两国的修辞研究者更多地关注和交流双方的修辞研究和实践，并通过我们的研究增进两国人民之间的了解和理解。

Contents

前　言 ·· i

Chapter One　Introduction to the Study ································· 1
  1.1　Introduction ·· 1
  1.2　Problem Statement: Reality of China's Copyright Protection
       versus the Expectations of the United States ···················· 2
  1.3　Western/Greco-Roman Rhetorical Tradition ···················· 15
  1.4　U.S. Cultural Values and Beliefs ·· 17
  1.5　Chinese Rhetorical Heritage ·· 19
  1.6　Chinese Cultural Values and Beliefs ····································· 21
  1.7　Global Copyright Practice and the U.S.-China Debate ········ 23
  1.8　Rhetoric: A General Definition and its Relatedness to the
       Project ·· 27
  1.9　Rhetoric and the U.S.-China Copyright Approaches:
       Meta-Methods ··· 30

1.10 Conclusion 31
Chapter Two   Methods 33
    2.1 Introduction 33
    2.2 Main Research Question and Sub-Questions 34
    2.3 Quantitative and Qualitative Methods versus Rhetorical Criticism 35
    2.4 Why Comparative Rhetorical Approach 38
    2.5 Cluster Analysis: An Approach to Articulate the Author's Intention on the Audience 41
    2.6 Intercultural Rhetoric/Communication: The Approach to Cultural Values and Beliefs as Well as Behaviors 45
    2.7 Marxist Criticism: An Ideological Approach to the U.S.-China Conflicts over Copyright Practice 50
    2.8 Researcher Role 53
    2.9 Research Materials 54
    2.10 Conclusion 62
Chapter Three   Rhetorical Tradtions and Western(U.S.)/ Chinese Legal (Copyright) Approaches—A Cluster Analysis 63
    3.1 Introduction 63
    3.2 Rule by Law or Rule by Man: The Concept of *Virtue*/*Ethos* in Early Greco/Roman and Chinese Rhetorical Traditions ... 64
    3.3 Plato's Concept of *Virtue* in *Protagoras* 66
    3.4 *Ethos* as Human Character in Aristotle's *On Rhetoric* 71

3.5 Cicero's *Ideal Orator* in *De Oratore* ·················· 76

3.6 Chinese Rhetorical Tradition: Confucianism and Daoism ·· 81

3.7 Western and Chinese Concept of *Virtue/Ethos* and its Potential Impact on U.S. and Chinese Legal (Copyright) Approaches: A Comparison and Contrast ············· 97

3.8 Conclusion ··· 101

Chapter Four   The Impact of Cultural Traditions on the U.S. and China Legal/Copyright Approaches—the Cultural Dimensions ·· 103

4.1 Introduction ··· 103

4.2. U.S. Cultural Dimensions: Cultural Values and Beliefs Revealed in the *Declaration of Independence and* the *U.S. Constitution* ·· 105

4.3 Universalism, Individualism, and Low Power Distance: U.S. Cultural Dimensions and Values and Beliefs ············· 108

4.4 Chinese Cultural Dimensions: Cultural Values and Beliefs Revealed in the *Constitution of the People's Republic of China* and Deng Xiaoping's *Southern Tour Speeches* ······ 115

4.5 Particularism, Collectivism, and High Power Distance: Chinese Cultural Dimensions and Values and Beliefs ······· 120

4.6 Cultural Dimensions and Their Potential Impact on the U.S.-China Copyright Approaches: A Comparison and Contrast ··· 130

4.7　Conclusion ·· 136

Chapter Five　The U.S. and Chinese Approaches to Copyright Practice—An Ideological Criticism ················ 137

5.1　Introduction ·· 137

5.2　Global Copyright Protection: From Internationalization to Globalization ·· 139

5.3　The U.S.-China Copyright Conflicts: The *1992 MOU* and the *1995 U.S.-China IP Agreement* ······················ 146

5.4　The Ideology of the Conflict: Implications for the U. S. and Chinese Copyright Approaches ····················· 161

5.5　Conclusion ·· 167

Chapter Six　Discussions and Conclusions ·························· 169

6.1　Introduction ·· 169

6.2　Summary of Research Results ······························· 170

6.3　Conclusions ·· 177

6.4　Recommendations for the Discipline and Policy Makers ··· 183

6.5　Limitations of the Study ······································ 189

6.6　Contributions ·· 190

References ·· 191

Chapter One

Introduction to the Study

1.1 Introduction

This book examines the U.S. and the Chinese approaches to copyright practice from a rhetorical perspective. Using theories and methods from comparative rhetoric, intercultural rhetoric/communication, and ideological criticism, I attempt to address the question: *In what ways do rhetorical and cultural traditions in the United States and China and global copyright practice impact the understanding and enforcement of copyright in their respective countries and in what ways are these expectations influential in U.S./China professional communication?* More specifically, I argue that the notions of *virtue/ethos* and related concepts in Western/U.S. and Chinese rhetorical traditions, cultural orientations, and global copyright practice reflect and affect the two cultures' approaches to copyright.

In this chapter, I present the dissonance between China's copyright reality and the United States' expectations as represented by existing research. I review the relevant literature to support the discussion and then develop the theoretical framework that guides this rhetorical examination.

1.2 Problem Statement: Reality of China's Copyright Protection versus the Expectations of the United States

Since its initiation of economic reform and open door policy in the late 1970s and early 1980s, China has started a profound economic and business communication with the Western world and the United States in particular, given that the U.S. is a major technology and information exporter and China an importer. In order to line up with international trade practice and gain its access to world market, as well as regulate domestic business operations, China passed numerous laws in the past two decades between the 1980s and 1990s (Alford, 1999; Tang, 2004). Included are the copyright law and implementation regulations that have been promulgated as a measure to protect the interests of inventors and authors, as well as to enhance intellectual and technological creations and innovations. Consequently, the U.S. is led to believe that with the copyright legislation and enforcement regulations that are developed mainly on Western legal conventions or under U.S. pressure (Yang, 2003; La Croix and Konan, 2002), China will offer a secure market for its products, particularly products of information and high technology where intellectual property laws are enacted.

The U.S. expectations for an ideal copyright protection in the Chinese market have good reasons. As an advanced capitalist economy that has developed a comprehensive copyright law and been relying on legal enforcement to conduct smooth business practice within the country since the eighteenth century, the U.S. believed that China's copyright laws would also prove to be a sound legal guarantee that assures the rights and interests for all copyright holders. Moreover, maintaining that foreign technology transfer also advances China's economic development (Marcus, 2000; Marcus, Dougherty, and Mertha, 1998), the U.S. expected that the Chinese government of every level would grant adequate attention to the administration of copyright laws when infringing happens. In the same way, the intellectual property (IP) legal enforcers, agencies and relevant organizations, and professionals would take effective enforcement actions on infringers.

However, China's copyright reality presents a big disparity from the U.S. expectations. Unauthorized dissemination of products prevail: music and movie CDs, DVDs, and computer software are sold in big shopping centers, on the street booths, and by street vendors, indicating a general ignorance of copyright law and the corresponding rules from the general public and a failure of adequate legal enforcement (Mertha, 2005; Alford, 1995; Bender, 2006). Consequently, the U.S. concluded that China provides a market of counterfeiting and piracy, and copyright law and its regulations are only laws on paper (Mertha, 2005; May, 2001; Sell, 1995; Alford,

1995).

The result of this disparity not only has rendered trade battles and lengthy negotiations between the two governments (Mathur, 2003; Yu, 2001; Roy, 2007), it also raised concerns and discussions from researchers, especially U.S. scholars, who offered their perspectives pertaining China's copyright protection issue. Most scholars (Mertha, 2005; Alford, 1995, 1999, 2002; Yang, 2003; Meyer, 2001) located major reasons that caused widespread piracy: the government's political/ideological priority and dysfunctional administration and unprofessional legal practice due to government interference, inadequate professional preparation, and power abuse. They argued:

- The Chinese government's priority has been on cracking down on anti-government/Communist Party publications and pornographical materials, while neglecting the protection of copyright.
- Departments responsible for copyright enforcement lack coordination and local governments are more interested in revenues infringing brings to local economy.
- China's legal practice lacks professionalism due to government interference with legal procedures, inadequate professional education, and power abuse.

Still others approached the issue from an economic perspective while they agree on the political and legal inadequacies involved in IP rights (IPRs) protection. For example, these researchers believed effective copyright/IP protection enhances China's economic development (Maskus, 2000; Maskus et. al., 1998) because strong copyright protection brings in more foreign direct investment.

Therefore, economists offer Chinese government measures and solutions that they believe will strengthen protection and urge China to take actions.

In order to provide better knowledge of current research on China's copyright issue, the following discussion reviews existing studies that focused on the political, legal, and economic aspects of China's copyright practice.

1.2.1 China's Copyright Issue: the Political Focus

Mertha (2005) and Alford (1995) first criticized China's administrative apparatus that manages and enforces copyright protection, asserting that it has been supine and ineffective. The reasons they gave are several. First, China's copyright regime emphasizes ideological control rather than copyright protection. Mertha observed that China's copyright bureaucracy is embedded within a system that prioritizes enforcement tasks on anti-government/communist party publications and pornography over intellectual property violations (2005), indicating China's political focus, even though the latter is also categorized as illegal publications. Here, he was referring to the Press and Publication Administration (PPA) to which the copyright bureaucracy is subjected and the governmental organ that concerns itself more with "cultural, ideological and value-laden media and is therefore involved in a more political sensitive environment" (p.133). In addition, copyright agencies received less support from the parent body in the aspects of personnel and budget support due to their insignificance in the PPA. In addition, there was a lack of common interest between the parent body and the branch when the former mainly focused on censorship and showed less interest in promoting the rights of the authors (Mertha, 2005; Wang, 2004) while the latter's task was to protect IPRs.

The emphasis on ideology and neglect of copyright protection also manifest themselves in the inadequacy of the enforcement administration. For example, Mertha found that instead of effective and sustainable enforcement procedures, the Chinese government initiated sporadic enforcement campaigns (which is a usual practice for the government when it promotes a certain policy or launches a movement) that always failed to achieve a long-term effect. According to Mertha, these campaigns were "incapable of responding swiftly to the operations of the pirates who were often scattered throughout a given geographical area, highly mobile, and prone to exploiting flexible and sophisticated 'exit strategies' to stay several steps ahead of authorities" (2005, p. 140).

Mertha is not the only one who had a problem with copyright protection in China about inadequate administrative attention to copyright enforcement. Many other specialists, Chinese and the U.S., (Alford, 1995; Shi, 2008; Maskus, Dougherty, and Mertha, 1998; Bettig, 1996; Holtz-Eakin, 2005; Wang, 2004) have also expressed their concerns with China's substandard administrative practice of copyright enforcement. For example, Shi identified counterfeiting and piracy as a by-product derived from a dysfunctional institutional regime (2008). Wang (2004) shared some of the points with Mertha, such as financial and personnel shortage of enforcement agencies due to inadequate support from the government, asserting that intellectual property right infringement prevailed in China and had caused even healthcare problems (p. 255).

Wang (2004) found out that the neglect of copyright enforcement in the administration was also caused by ineffective coordination between ministerial departments that are in charge of the copyright matter in particular sectors. In addition, she noticed that ineffective enforcement happened in lower level governments that prioritized revenues infringers brought to the local economy. This is because economic increase is viewed as local governments' administrative achievement which will enhance career promotion and is regarded as officials' allegiance to the country and loyalty to the Communist Party as a result of their carrying out the Party's Policies. Such an approach to copyright/IPR protection hinders effective enforcement. Therefore, Wang (2004) maintained that although China had established a sophisticated framework of IP protection, it is "flashy but without substance" because the enforcement has been inadequate (p. 254). Feder (1996) even used a famous Chinese saying to describe the reality and express his disappointment with the situation: "you can lead a horse to the water but can't make it drink"(p.223)

Admittedly, political priority in China's legal practice is never a new thing. Rather, it has been an inherent feature of China's legal tradition (Cai, 1999; Glen, 2009; Potter, 2001). Like what Ren (1997) reported:

> Established government institutions and the stipulated rule of law may have been changed [in China] ... However, the distribution and penetration of the state's power into social fabric are far more subtle and complicated than understanding institutional reorganization and legislative stipulation. Over the centuries, Chinese leaders, regardless

of the philosophical belief and political appeal, have displayed a consistent commitment to a model with the state's strong will in controlling and ordering society (p. 1).

The current government, like all its predecessors, continues to view political control as administrative priority regardless of its economic and political reform. Everything else is less significant.

1.2.2 China's Copyright Issue: the Legal Focus

Apart from the factors of political priority that includes dysfunctional administration and local protectionism, many researchers brought a legal perspective into the debate. Although a few researchers recognized China's progress in copyright legislation and implementation (Peerenboom, 1999, 2007; Yang, 2003; Feng and Wei, 2002), the majority of them who focused on the implementation "grudgingly give China a modicum of credit for making some improvements" (Oksenberg, Potter, and Abnett, 1996, Alford, 1995) and uniformly maintained that China's copyright enforcement is rudimentary and has failed to live up to prior treatises to police piracy stipulated by U.S. and/ international copyright laws, and bilateral agreements (Wang, 2004; Maskus, 2000; Mertha, 2005; Alford, 1995 and more). Most researchers who reviewed China's copyright issue from a legal perspective contributed copyright protection failure to China's unprofessional legal practice due to government interference (Alford, 2002; Mertha, 2004; Ren, 1997, p. 8), inadequate professional education, and corruption in the profession (Alford, 2002). They found that court decisions are partial, unjust, and lack independence. Many times, the ruling party, represented by officials, is above the law:

> The Communist Party, which is not only the nation's leading repository of political power, but which also continues to be its single most consequential actor economically and in many other respects, remains above the state's law, both as a formal and as a practical matter...(Alford, 2002, p. 7)

It is normal that authorities of higher levels who demand or are demanded by more powerful people, relatives, friends, or interest partners to interfere in order to "correct" a judicial or public decision. Ren thus concluded, "... though China might have created what can be called laws, they are often sidestepped by the government officials" (1997, p.2). In many local areas, party authorities consider themselves representing or are above the law. "The sky is high and the emperor is far away." This popular Chinese saying portrays the mentality of law abusers who take advantage of their power fearlessly for personal gains.

The man-rules-over-the-law reality confirms Wang's findings regarding local protectionism (2004). When copyright violations occur, local officials, instead of taking measures to protect copyright, they are more interested in revenues brought about by the businesses that produce or deal with unauthorized products. Therefore, these researchers believed the interference with or in-action of local governments toward copyright infringement raises a bigger challenge to the already ineffective copyright enforcement.

Researchers also believed China's inexperience in IPR legislation and implementation constitutes the country's unprofessional legal/copyright practice (Wang, 2004; Ren, 1997; Alford, 1999, 2002). Profound IP practice did not exist in China before late 1970s and early 1980s. As a matter of fact, anything that could be considered law by the Western standards is a very recent event in China (Ren, 1997, p. 8; Alford, 1999, 2002). From 1987 to 1992, China issued more than 2,000 laws, statutes, amendments, and decrees, exceeding the total numbers of laws enacted in its first three decades under the Communist rule since 1949 (Ren, 1997, p. 2). This fast pace in legal development, on one hand, indicates China's legal development in the past thirty years; on the other hand, it implies China's gap in this respect and the challenges it faces to raise public legal and copyright awareness within such a short time. In addition, IP practice is complicated and challenging even for experienced practitioners. For example, the U.S. status as a major piracy country in the world lasted for more than a century. Even though the U.S. issued its copyright act as early as in 1790, it did not provide copyright protection for foreign works until a hundred years later and free riding European authors had been very popular (Yu, 2003; Varian, 2005).

The unprofessionalism is also caused by inadequate education and training of legal professionals. In a little over a generation from the late 1970s, "the Chinese bar has expanded from 3,000 members to more than 175,000, with the state continuing to make noises about its plans for China to have 300,000 lawyers by the end of the current decade" (Alford, 2002, p. 7) to meet legal demand brought about by the increasing economic development. This fast production causes suspicion with the quality of the professionals. For example, veterans from the military without any professional training are often assigned legal enforcement positions such as in police department, the courts, and procuratorate offices in the profession. In most cases, these people do not have the qualifications that meet the criteria for legal profession. Alford (2002) also found informal processes are common in the legal, professional, and formal procedures, which allows flexibility that ignores laws and rules, adding to the already administrative recourse feature of China's legal practice.

Corruption of the legal professionals causes ineffective IPRs enforcement. It creates erosion of trust in the law and fearlessness of consequent legal punishment (Alford, 2002). In his research, Alford reported that some lawyers even use litigation as a pretext for bribery (2002, p. 9) to benefit from the current distribution of power (p. 14). Consequently, "Resort to law and lawyers remains very much the exception in Chinese affairs both large and small" (2002, p. 7).

Researchers, who viewed China's copyright issue from a legal perspective, maintained unanimously that China's legal practice in general is unprofessional due to inexperience, lack of independence, inadequate education, and corruption all of which cause ineffective legal enforcement.

1.2.3 China's Copyright Issue: the Economic Focus

Other researchers responded to China's copyright issue from an economic perspective. While acknowledging the issue involves political and legal factors, they mainly attempted to convince the Chinese government and the general public that stronger copyright/IPR protection would promote further economic development in the aspect of domestic technological innovation and foreign direct investment (FDI) (Maskus, Dougherty and Mertha 1998; Branstetter, Fisman, Foley and Saggi, 2005; Yang, 2003).

Maskus, Dougherty, and Mertha (1998) resonated with researchers who believed that China's problematic copyright protection is caused by the government's ineffective administration and enforcement. However, as economists, they explored further into how effective enforcement of IPRs would impact China's economic development positively. They held that a favorable IPRs environment will enhance economic development through stimulating inventions and innovations, deepening market, assuring quality, and diffusing international and domestic knowledge in China, as well as meeting Chinese needs through global research and development (1998, p. 5-15). In other words, an unfavorable IPRs environment would hinder China's economic development.

Many researchers sided with Maskus, Dougherty, and Mertha over the positive effect of strong copyright/IPRs enforcement for developing economies such as China (Branstetter, L., Fisman R., Foley, C. F. and Saggi, K., 2005). For example, Branstetter et. al. contended:

> [S]trengthening IP rights in developing countries leads to increased foreign direct investment (FDI) in the developed countries, as firms in developed countries shift product to their affiliates in the developing countries resulting in accelerating industrial development. Additionally, the developed countries will reallocate their sources to research and development, thus drive an increase in the global rate of innovation (quoted from abstract).

Maskus (2000) also emphasized that in semi-industrialized developing economies like China where domestic interest in advancing IPR protection is emerging, imitative skills could be successfully transformed into effective technical capabilities for legal adaptation to foreign technologies (p.191). Therefore, he asserted that "improving IPRs...could not only attract markedly more investment and technology licensing from abroad, it could also provide important incentives for domestic entrepreneurs to build new firms and market new products" (p.191). Yang agreed that IPR protection is the key to providing investors and technology owners with a secure environment, and thereby to attracting capital and technology (2003).

Admittedly, criticism of China's inadequacy of copyright protection is not unfounded fabrication and effective copyright protection has positive effects on China's economic development. The political, legal, and economic points of views portray the truthful reality. Yet, copyright protection as a global practice imported to China, represents a much more complicated issue than simply connecting it with political priority and administrative dysfunction, ineffective legal enforcement, and economic enhancement. In other words, examining the issue from these perspectives paints part of the picture of China's copyright protection issue. It misses the important spectrum that copyright practice is a foreign practice newly imported to China and is laden with Western beliefs and values. Consequently, Chinese understanding of and approach to copyright carries particular social, historic, and cultural influences that differ from what the Western/U.S. expects to be adequate protection.

More specifically, current research on China's copyright practice ignores the fact that individuals' approach to formal laws such as IPRs is culturally bound, suggesting what one culture believes to be morally and legally acceptable also depends on the cultural environment. How individuals of a given culture approach copyright practice is connected with their rhetorical and cultural background. What a person learns affects what he does. Without a careful consideration of the rhetorical and cultural factors, current studies provide partial information of China's copyright issue and reduce their research to one piece of a puzzle when they fail to offer a fuller picture of the situation. Here, I argue not that the perspectives are wrong because they all accommodated understanding of China's copyright issue in the debate. Rather, I argue it is a complex issue and a broader scope of factors should be considered.

Therefore, this project seeks to complement existing researches in the U.S.-China debate over China's copyright practice. Based on the assumption that rhetorical, cultural, and global copyright movement together reflect and impact a culture's approach to legal practice, the project integrates into the discussion of cross-cultural rhetorical and cultural traditions as well as the movement of global copyright practice exemplified by the U.S.-China copyright conflict. This meta-method represents a rhetorical approach that has not been adopted much in the fields of IPRs or rhetoric and professional communication. My goal for this approach is to add another piece to our puzzle and broaden the scope of research in the two fields. It also serves a more practical purpose to provide knowledge for practitioners and policy makers who are engaged in U.S.-China business and professional communication.

Consequently, the rest of the chapter stresses a description of the theoretical framework. It introduces U.S. and Chinese rhetorical traditions, their separate cultural values and beliefs, as well as the impact of global copyright practice in the example of the U.S.-China conflict through the analytical methods of cluster analysis, cultural dimensions, and Marxist criticism that I examine closely in next chapter.

1.3 Western/Greco-Roman Rhetorical Tradition

Western rhetorical tradition as represented primarily by Plato, Aristotle, and Cicero I choose to study in the project, emphasizes rhetoric's social functions to influence individuals and shape social order (Bizzell and Herzberg, 2001; Herrick, 2005). While offering various persuasive strategies in the rhetorical process, these rhetoricians all valued the significance of virtuous quality of a persuasive or ideal orator in persuasion that intends for the above-mentioned functions. Plato, Aristotle, and Cicero identified the quality as *virtue*, *ethos*, or *knowledge* of all subjects and extended the concept to legal compliance of individuals.

Western rhetorical practice flourished in the primitive democracy of the ancient Athens where public speeches were common in the courts of law, at legislative assemblies, and at ceremonial occasions, three rhetorical settings where speakers provided either true *knowledge/justice* or falseness/injustice (*episteme* or belief) to the audiences depending on their purpose and ability (*Gorgias*; *Protagoras*). Therefore, Plato stressed the importance of *virtue* of speakers who educated people and influenced decision making in the legal, legislative, and political domain for individual citizens, the public, and the state. As a result, ethical rhetorical practice is particularly important. He criticized the sophists who he believed were practicing unethical rhetoric by clever talk to manipulate public opinion (*doxa*) (*Protagoras*, p. 452). He stressed that their practice did not offer *justice* or true *knowledge* (*episteme*) but about *justice* and *knowledge*. Plato claimed that rhetoric, to be a true art (*techne*), should aim at the well being of individuals and of the city-state (*polis*). In doing so, he associated rhetorical practice with establishing *justice* and *virtue* in the individuals that included observing the law, social justice, democracy, and stability of the society as a whole.

Aristotle also acknowledged the ethical purpose of rhetoric and argued that "knowing rhetoric is useful in order to ensure that just and true ideas prevail over unjust and false ones"| (Herrick, 2005, p. 77). This interpretation recognizes the social function and ultimate goal of rhetoric to inform, persuade, and influence individuals by cultivating *virtue* in the individuals and to establish an orderly and democratic society. Thus, Aristotle directly connected moral responsibilities of the speaker and individuals to public interest. He pointed out that *ethos,* the virtuous character of the speaker, when combined with logos and pathos, constitutes a rhetorical strategy for persuasion.

Cicero claimed that effective rhetorical practice combines moral science or wisdom and eloquence that helped individuals to sustain civil rights by means of defending himself and maintaining the order of the state. He held that demonstrating one's good character (Plato's *virtue* and Aristotle's *ethos*) through rhetoric was vital to a successful orator (Herrick, 2005, p. 94). In achieving his moral duty as an *ideal orator*, the speaker should command knowledge of the subject he addresses and particularly of public laws. He truly believed that the orator could teach men to "seek...good reputation (*dignitas*), *virtue* and right and honest labour", and only civil rights could "dominate greed and protect property" (*De Oratore*, 2.21) and keep social order.

Regardless of their similar and different interpretations of *virtue/ethos*, there is one thing that Plato, Aristotle, and Cicero shared and is most relevant to my topic of copyright practice. They all attached legal aspect to the concept of *virtue/ethos* and believed that legal awareness secures social order, *justice*, democracy, and protection of individual properties and happiness.

1.4 U.S. Cultural Values and Beliefs

The U.S. culture carries the legacy of Greco-Roman/Western rhetorical tradition and has adapted it to the specific U.S. political and social contexts to emphasize especially rhetoric's significance in forming individuality and establishing the relationship between individual citizens and the state. While U.S. rhetorical practice recognizes Western classical rhetoric to be the study of possible means of persuasion that informs, convinces, and shapes the human mind in different rhetorical settings, it strongly stresses rhetoric's functions to defend individual interests, maintain civil rights, as well as shape the American culture. More specifically, rhetorical practice in the U.S. has been adopted as its ultimate goals to advocate independence, freedom, equality, and democracy. Such characteristics saturate the U.S. cultural values and beliefs which become unique cultural orientations that impact the country's interaction with other cultures in different contexts which may include the U.S. global copyright effort. I identify these cultural orientations as universalism, individualism, and low power distance. They are manifest both in the *Declaration of Independence* (the *Declaration*) and the *U.S. Constitution* that I study.

The *Declaration of Independence* identifies "life, liberty, and the pursuit of happiness" as unalienable and god-given rights for all individuals in the American colonies. As one of the most important artifacts in the U.S. rhetorical practice, it portrays the essence of U.S. values and beliefs. The *Declaration* lists colonial grievances against the British king to legitimize the war of independence for freedom, liberty, and equal rights for individuals, which the U.S. holds as natural rights. The notion of natural rights intersects with natural law/*justice* that Plato and Aristotle had frequently mentioned in their works and that Cicero attached to individuals who were obliged to contribute to the general good of the larger society.

The *U.S. Constitution* continues the mission of the *Declaration of Independence,* promising to "establish *justice*...promote the general welfare...and to secure the Blessings of Liberty..." (Preamble). The notion of natural right and law or *justice* in the *U.S. Constitution* indicates the effort of the framework to balance power between government bodies for the purpose of preventing power abuse and tyranny of which the U.S. had previously accused Great Britain of. It specifies the powers and duties of each government branch and the relationship of the federal government with the states and citizens of the United States. The articulation of the natural rights is specific and profound. It not only includes freedom of speech, religion, and assembly, but also promises to protect private property right (The *U.S. Constitution*) and the authorship of literary works which later is defined as copyright the U.S. strives to promote unalterably in China in the past two decades.

The U.S. culture highlights individuality, democracy, freedom, and independence. Such values and beliefs tend to emphasize rule of law, individuality, and equal treatment. Reflected in legal approach and copyright practice will mean more public respect for individual private property rights, effective law enforcement, and an equal playing field for individuals.

1.5 Chinese Rhetorical Heritage

China's rhetorical practice, of both ancient and modern times, has a continuing influence on the Chinese view of the world and their style of communication which includes how they understand the notions of individual obligations, rights, and private property ownership related to copyright. Like their Greek counterparts, ancient Chinese philosophers and rhetoricians in the fifth century B. C. E. practiced rhetoric to influence and shape people and the context in which they lived. Many concepts in Chinese rhetorical works center on language, persuasion, and argumentation that formulate the Chinese rhetorical experience (Lu, 1998, p. 3; Zheng and Zong, 1998) "words, ideas, and concepts are passed on and inherited, and manifest themselves as part of the Chinese cultural entities" (Cao, p. 22). For example, the concept of *virtue* was even more emphasized by Confucianism and Daoism, the two major schools of thought that permeate the Chinese life. Although the Confucians and Daoists interpreted *virtue* differently, they both viewed it as human moral quality that regulated individuals' behavior and ordered society. They believed that individuals' moral cultivation, or following the law of nature without contention, helped individuals achieve virtuous qualities that not only improve individuals as persons but also eventually shaped societal order with a better result than formal laws.

Confucianism represents the mainstream of Chinese moral philosophy that intertwines with its rhetorical concepts which emphasize human virtuousness more than anything else. According to Confucius, benevolence (*ren*) is the key to cultivating human morality and restoring and maintaining social order. The Confucians believed that if individuals are benevolent and kind to each other, families will be in harmony. If families are in harmony, the entire society will be in good order and prosper. Based on this belief, the Confucians further urged the state leaders to govern their states and people with benevolence to sustain their reign. They pointed out that formal laws were a coercive force which may have effectively prevented people from committing crimes, but they could not convince and motivate men to really become virtuous individuals (*The Analects; Mencius*). The solution Confucius offered is a hierarchical relationship in the family, the guild, and the state that assures individuals will understand their own obligations toward other people and society and their superiors. Mencius particularly stressed the significance of benevolent governance. The Confucians held that only when individuals become benevolent themselves through following the rituals established by ancient sages would society enjoy the harmony between heaven and humans.

Opposite of the Confucian cultivation of individual benevolence, Lao Zi's representation of Daoism considered humans slaves of their selfishness and as being controlled by their desire. Totally refuting the Confucian approach to social problems, Lao Zi proposed that men should discard their selfish desire and greed through meditation, simple life, and non-action (*Dao De Jing*), which he believed to be human *virtue* (*de*). Only through giving up individuality would society restore order and establish a harmonious relationship in conformity with the Way of nature (*dao*).

Although Confucius, Mencius, and Lao Zi provided different interpretations of human *virtue*, they all privileged sacrifice of individuality for public interest and rejected formal laws, believing that individual awareness of *virtue* was the ultimate solution to social issues. Such values reflected in copyright practice may be a common neglect of formal laws and tolerance of rampant piracy due to the belief that harsher rules force people to conform to legal practice but do not really convince them to be better citizens.

1.6 Chinese Cultural Values and Beliefs

China's rhetorical practice bears a direct effect on Chinese cultural values and beliefs that shape how the Chinese view and interact with the world around them. The Confucian and Daoist emphasis on the cultivation of individual *virtue* through observing hierarchical relationships and eliminating personal desires leads to strong values of collectivism, individuals' obligations, public ownership, unequal distribution of power, etc. at the sacrifice of individuality, which illustrates cultural dimensions of particularism, collectivism, and high power distance.

One of the most significant Chinese values is collectivism that prioritizes public and state interest over individual interests. For instance, the *Constitution of the People's Republic of China* (*China's Constitution*), one of the two artifacts I have chosen to investigate for cross-cultural rhetoric/communication comparison, identifies collective and state ownerships as the nation's economic system. Such a system favors collective interest and requires individuals to surrender to public benefits at their personal sacrifice. Another example of the collectivistic cultural value associated with China's rhetorical tradition is the cultivation of nationalism which calls the public to remember the country's contemporary history characterized by foreign invasions and domestic upheavals. Such contextual information in the *Constitution* aims at a patriotic education for the public. The stress of collective and public interest runs into conflict with copyright protection that emphasizes individual private benefits and rights and brings about public ignorance of copyright protection and high piracy, flexibilities in law enforcement, and sacrifice of individual interest.

In addition, hierarchy represents a significant cultural value that China embraces. From an individual level, the *Constitution* explicitly requires adult children to pay reciprocal respect to their elder parents. From a national level, both the *Constitution* and *Deng's Speeches* legitimize one-party dictatorship that deprives any other political entities of the right to lead governance. Such a practice claims that social harmony and national integrity are to be achieved under the sole rule of the Communist Party of China without contention. It illustrates the impact of the Confucian and Daoist propositions of maintaining social order through hierarchical relationships and non-contention which may result in the abuse of power by influential people, social inequality, and neglect of individuality. In the case of copyright protection, government officials or people in higher political and social positions may use their power to interfere with enforcement actions and judicial procedures for personal gains which definitely impact copyright enforcement.

1.7 Global Copyright Practice and the U.S.-China Debate

The above discussion emphasized rhetorical notions of *virtue/ethos* and cultural dimensions as well as their potential influence on how the two cultures approach formal laws, individual obligations/rights, and ownership and copyright. This part of the chapter introduces the copyright debate between the U.S. and China from an ideological perspective in the context of copyright/IP internationalization and globalization movement.

Global copyright practice has evolved from internationalization to globalization (Drahos, 2002; Braithwaite and Drahos, 2000; May, 1995). The first stage took place in major European countries and produced the *Berne Convention for the Protection of Literary and Artistic Works* (the *Berne Convention*) which standardized international copyright legislations across national borders. First spread to developed countries and then moved to developing nations, the *Berne Convention* was adopted in Berne, Switzerland in September 1886 and is the representative product of copyright internationalization. The founding countries established criteria of protection and controlled standard setting based on their social and cultural situations. These countries, France, Germany, Spain and the U.K., recognized the need to protect authored works from international piracy and publishing, asserting that authors, domestic and foreign, should maintain their personality and integrity, which is the moral right (the *Berne Convention*, 6bis) and right to the economic interest in their creations. While the *Berne Convention* provides a minimum standard of protection, it allows individual countries flexibilities to adjust to always higher protection standards in their own countries and to protect authorship and copyrights from free-riding in the member countries.

Globalization, closely tied to the increasingly globalized economy, represents the second stage of world copyright practice which produced the significant *Trade Related Intellectual Property Agreement* (*TRIPS Agreement*) to not only maintain the principles of the *Berne Convention* but extend copyright protection to all trade related copyright issues as well as have a binding force for all WTO members. In the establishment of the *TRIPS Agreement*, developed countries, the U.S. in particular, dominated standard setting while developing countries made great reconciliations due to their dependency on the U.S. market and fear of consequent punishment caused by IPRs violations (Sell, 1995; Yu, 2002). The *TRIPS Agreement* not only broadens the scope of IPRs protection and binds all WTO members, it also symbolizes the U.S. hegemonic control over IPR practice in world trade which reduces developing countries to a disadvantageous position.

The *TRIPS Agreement*, while maintaining the standard of the *Berne Convention*, connects IPRs with the world trading system, thus broadens the scope of IPR protection. The U.S. convinced the members at the 1994 *Uruguay Round of the General Agreement on Tariffs and Trade* (GATT) to sign the agreement through aggressive lobbyism by its big businesses that have high IP profiles (Drahos, 2002; May, 1995). These multinational companies attempt to globalize IPRs regulations, protect their interests, and gain more access to world markets (Drahos, 1995). The most significant feature of the TRIPS is its general principles dealing with "domestic procedures and remedies for the enforcement of the IPRs" as well as its ability to make WTO member disputes related to IPRs subject to the WTO's settlement procedure (*TRIPS Agreement*, 1995; Drahos, 2002, 2000; May, 1995). As a consequence, developed countries that are mainly technology exporters secured more control over intellectual properties and IPR-related trades than less developed/developing countries that are mainly importers of technology. Also, it allows developed countries to interfere with IPR legislative procedures and enforcement implementations in developing countries. In such circumstances, the interest of developing countries with regard to IPRs is mostly ignored and marginalized.

Although all members signed the *Berne Convention* and the *TRIPS Agreement*, developing countries have a problem with maintaining conformity to the standards. This is because the standards did not consider the circumstance and ability of developing countries when most of these developing countries had limited experience in copyright legislation and protection, as many had never exercised a meaningful sovereignty over setting copyright standards (Drahos, 2002, p. 7) nor had an adequate copyright law. The international and global copyright system is run "to suit the [economic] interests of copyright exporters [and] each successive revision ... brought with it a higher set of copyright standards" (Drahos, 2002, p. 8) that do not address the national interests of the former colonies and other developing countries. Consequently, the movement of copyright internationalization and globalization presents an ideological practice that involves conflict of interests and cultural orientations toward world copyright practice. Such a clash is evidenced in the U.S.-China debates in the early1990s.

The U.S.-China conflicts over China's copyright issue exemplify an ideological encounter that reflects and affects the two cultures' approaches to copyright practice. In the conflicts, the U.S. controlled the negotiation process and set protection standards while China was in subordination. In the two settlements that produced the *1992 Memorandum of Understanding* between the two governments (the *1992 MOU*) and the *U.S.-China IP Agreement* (the *1995 IP Agreement*) I chose to examine, the U.S. set deadlines for China to adjust its copyright laws to international practice, accede to international copyright conventions, and enforce protection plans and actions. China was also made to meet the standards and open more market for U.S. copyrighted materials or China would have to face billion dollars worth of trade sanctions. Both agreements are one-sided treatises highlighting China's obligations as opposed to a few of the U.S. duties, indicating an imbalance of power in conflict settlement. China yielded to the U.S. domination because of its dependency on the U.S. market for its export goods (U.S. Census Bureau), demand for technology transfer (Marcus, 1999; Yang, 2003), as well as concerns of trade retaliations worth a billion dollars (*USTR Special Report*, 199-1994; Yu, 2002). As a result, the bilateral consensus embodied the elements of domination, reconciliation, negotiation, and coercion, etc. which are characteristics of the Marxist approach to examining rhetorical and cultural artifacts.

The U.S.-China copyright conflicts took place in the context of the internationalization and globalization of IPR practice. They illustrate the U.S. effort to promote copyright protection in China and conflicting values, ideals, objectives, cultural and political meanings (Hall, 2001; Storey, 2001). They also demonstrate the force of mutual benefit and interdependency that allows the existence of a "prevailing structure of power" (Hall, 2001, p. 104).

1.8 Rhetoric: A General Definition and its Relatedness to the Project

Rhetoric is "...the faculty of discovering all of the available means of persuasion in any given case" (*On Rhetoric*, I. 2.1355b). This classical Aristotecian definition embraces the use of language and the concept of choice. Many modern researchers, such as I. A. Richards, Kenneth Burke, and Chaim Perelman, added their interpretations while paying special attention to rhetoric's function to inform, persuade, shape our thoughts, as well as change the context in which we live (Herrick, 2005; Bizzell and Herzberg, 2001). George Kennedy (1998), for example, compared rhetorics in different cultures and concluded that rhetorical practice is universal, but it also demonstrates distinctive cultural features. Under such circumstances, rhetoric's function in different cultures remains the same, aiming at informing epistemology, persuading and influencing changes and decisions, and shaping thoughts and behavior. In other words, it changes people at both individual and national levels. At the same time, rhetorical perspectives employed in different cultures vary due to cultural uniqueness. Such features of rhetoric provide relevance to this study that highlights a rhetorical analysis of U.S. and Chinese approaches to copyright practice.

Based on Aristotle's definition, I. A. Richards defined language (which is always rhetorical) as "an instrument for the promotion of purposes" (Bizzell and Herzberg, 2001, p. 1271). Chaim Perelman best summarized the purpose of rhetoric is to "intensify an adherence to values, to create a disposition to act, and finally to bring people to act" (quoted in Golden, Berquist, and Coleman, 1983, p. 6). Burke's function of rhetoric echoed with, combined, and enhanced the nature of language and purpose of rhetoric through his articulation of the function of language. He maintained that language uses symbols to shape and change human beings and their context. Furthermore, he hoped that rhetoric could be harnessed to move human beings in the direction of cooperation and ultimately of peace. These Western ideas resonate with what their Chinese counterparts have been practicing with language use, even though the Chinese never developed rhetoric into a separate discipline or conceptualized it in the way the ancient Greeks did. The Chinese also have "a well-developed sense of the power and impact of language in their social, political, and individual lives" (Lu, 1998, p. 3). For instance, the *Analects,* as a work of ancient Chinese rhetoric that intended moral education, had been used as a required textbook in grade schools and an artifact for scholarly research for around two thousand years for the purpose of shaping both individuals and social order.

Although rhetorical practices in Western/U.S. and Chinese cultures have similar social functions, they are endowed with unique characteristics specific to their particular political, social, and cultural contexts (Kennedy, 1998; Lu, 1998). Based on this assumption, my project first discusses social functions of rhetoric. I adopt Kennedy's (1998) comparative rhetoric to reveal both similar and different features of Western/U.S. and Chinese rhetorical traditions that a non-comparative study may not be able to accomplish in its own context (p. 1). I adapt Kennedy's first and the fourth objectives into the following list to suit my research:

- Identify and analyze rhetorical notions that Western/U.S. and Chinese cultures might share or are unique to separate cultures.
- Examine the association of these rhetorical notions with copyright approach and their possible influence.

The assumption I make behind the choice is based on the accepted knowledge that rhetoric is universal but culturally different; it influences thought and shapes behavior in its specific cultural contexts. My discussion emphasizes the uniqueness while recognizing universal concept(s) that together contribute to the two cultures' perspectives of formal laws, ownership, and individual obligations and rights relevant to their approaches to copyright practice.

1.9 Rhetoric and the U.S.-China Copyright Approaches: Meta-Methods

Rhetoric's functions to inform, persuade, and shape individuals and society is closely associated with cultural values and beliefs that regulate individuals' thought patterns and decision-making in a given culture. This connection presents itself in artifacts cultures produce (Foss, 2004) and informs the theoretical framework and the meta-methods I use for the study. Global copyright promotion in China is rhetorical and cultural, as well as laden with and responded to by values and beliefs of the promoters and the receivers.

Therefore, the project adopts rhetorical criticism that combines Meta approaches: cluster analysis, intercultural rhetoric/communication, and Marxist method of ideological criticism. It first compares and contrasts key notions that connect Western and Chinese views of formal legal practice and social order, the sense of individuals' social obligations and rights, property, and ownership, which are the notions that I believe to be relevant to copyright approach. Next, the project examines and compares consequent cultural dimensions, specifying the orientations of universalism (communitarianism) versus particularism, individualism versus collectivism, and low versus high power distance. These dimensions reflect U.S. and Chinese values and beliefs related to the two cultures' legal and copyright approach. Lastly, the discussion focuses on the ideological aspect of global copyright practice in the historical context of IPR/copyright internationalization and globalization by introducing Marxist criticism and using the U.S.-China debate as an example.

The purpose of the analysis aims to complement existing understandings of global IPR practice. In addition, the study attempts to fill the gap in the field of rhetoric and professional communication that has produced limited study on the topic of copyright debate and provides informed knowledge about cross-cultural communication for policy makers.

1.10 Conclusion

This chapter articulated the problem statement by describing the dissonance between the U.S. expectations of China's copyright enforcement and the reality of ineffective protection. Then, it reviewed existing literature on China's copyright (IP) issue focused on the political, legal, and the economic perspectives and portrayed briefly earlier and later Western/U.S. and Chinese rhetorical practice and cultural factors. Next, the chapter described the U.S.-China copyright conflicts in the context of copyright/IPR internationalization and globalization which may reflect and impact the two cultures' view of formal laws and copyright practice. I grounded the study in the approach of rhetorical criticism, specifically, cluster analysis, intercultural rhetoric/communication, and Marxist criticism.

In Chapter Two I describe the methods: cluster analysis, cultural orientations, and Marxist criticism, selection of rhetorical artifacts, and analysis of artifacts. In Chapters Three, Four, and Five, I discuss the artifacts through multiple lenses of the theoretical frame, that is, cluster analysis, cultural variability, and Marxist approach. In Chapter Six, I summarize and discuss these findings and implications for the field of rhetoric and professional communication, particularly communication between the U.S. and China.

Chapter Two

Methods

2.1 Introduction

In Chapter One, I presented the dissonance between China's copyright reality and the United State's expectation as represented by existing research. I also described briefly the current copyright protection issue in China. Next, to address the problem caused by the dissonance, I developed a theoretical framework first by reviewing current studies conducted mainly by western scholars, particularly of those based in the United States, who offer political, economic, and legal perspectives pertaining to China's copyright issue. Then, I laid out the rhetorical and cultural background of the two cultures and the development of global copyrights protection. I also described briefly the academic and professional significance of this study and overviewed my methodology.

In this chapter, I turn to the research question and then concentrate on methods of inquiry. Here, I first describe the methods of comparing and contrasting rhetorical and cultural traditions. Next, I contextualize U.S.-China debate over China's piracy issue in copyright internationalization and globalization which influences the two cultures' separate approaches to copyright practice and formal laws. I also discuss the research materials that I call rhetorical texts/artifacts, explain briefly the sections or themes of my focus, and clarify the reasons for my choices. Then, I argue why the methods are a more appropriate approach than:

- Quantitative or qualitative approaches
- Non-comparative method
- A single method that emphasizes only one culture or one aspect of copyright issue

Lastly, I elaborate on the relevance of the chosen artifacts to the study and portray my role as a researcher.

2.2 Main Research Question and Sub-Questions

The dissonance described in the problem statement, the research gap in existing investigations, and my own knowledge about China's reality of copyright practice generate several concerns and questions about the U.S.-China copyright issue. While this project attempts to answer the main question: *In what ways do rhetorical and cultural traditions in the U.S. and China as well as copyright globalization impact understanding and enforcement of copyright in their respective countries and in what ways are these implications influential in U.S.-China professional communication?* The following sub-questions will also guide the inquiry:

- How do the U.S. and Chinese rhetorical and cultural traditions shape the two cultures' assumptions of law, ownership, morality and ethics, obligations, responsibilities, and rights which are relevant to the concept of copyright?
- How does U.S. and Chinese cultures negotiate between their assumptions of copyright with the ideologies of global copyright practice originated from the West?

2.3 Quantitative and Qualitative Methods versus Rhetorical Criticism

Conventional quantitative and qualitative methods seem inappropriate methods for this project due to the distinctive features of the research process of a rhetorical analysis. According to Creswell, "the knowledge that develops through the quantitative method is based on careful observation and measurement of the objective reality that exists out there in the world" (2005, p. 7). Consequently, the researcher will "develop numeric measures of observations and study the behavior of individuals" (Creswell, 2005, p. 7). Qualitative research, on the other hand, is naturalistic, descriptive, and inductive. It concerns process rather than simply outcomes or products and participants' perspectives (Bogdan and Biklen, 2003). Among these features, it is particularly distinctive of qualitative research that researchers mainly rely on field observations, open-ended interviews, public and private documents, and audiovisual materials for data collecting (Creswell, 2005. p. 17, 19, and 186-187).

This project focuses on the historical, social, cultural, and ideological situations that contribute to the shaping of individuals' behavior toward copyright practice at a cultural/national level rather than quantifying a certain behavior or relying on observations of or interviews with participants. Rhetorical criticism allows me to examine meaningful symbols for their potential influence on what people think and how they act with respect to copyright practice. Foss (2004) proposes that rhetorical criticism "is designed for the systematic investigation and explanation of symbolic acts and artifacts for the purpose of understanding rhetorical process" (p. 6). She further identifies three dimensions for this approach: systematic analysis, acts and artifacts as the objects of criticism, and understanding rhetorical processes as the purpose of criticism (p. 6-7). Systematic analysis involves conscious and focused investigation of both the discursive and the non-discursive symbols. It is a process through which the rhetorician becomes "more sophisticated and discriminating in explaining ... and understanding symbols and our responses to them" (Foss, 2004, p. 7). Symbolic acts and artifacts are objects of investigation in rhetorical criticism. Critics prefer to locate artifacts of the acts because artifacts are "tangible evidence" that are more accessible than acts.

In critiquing U.S. and Chinese copyright approaches rhetorically, specific behavior toward copyright, for example, respect or infringement, can be considered as symbolic acts that are "fleeting" and "ephemeral"; however, rhetorical artifacts that reflect and influence how individuals' perspectives of copyright are comparatively tangible. The third dimension, understanding rhetorical process allows the researcher to examine how particular symbols work (Foss, 2004, p. 7). This dimension first allows me to locate the clustering terms related to the notions of formal laws, ownership, obligations, individual rights, and morality ethics which I consider relevant to the copyright issue. Then, I can explore their meanings and influence on how people view laws, which consequently relates to their behavior toward copyright protection.

Rhetorical criticism, as a critical research method, recognizes human acts, knowledge, and understanding of their surroundings are socially constructed and recorded in the symbols they create (Foss, 2004; Golden, Berquist, and Coleman, 1983). This method allows me to examine the U.S. and Chinese approaches to copyright by taking into account "historical and cultural norms that operate in the individuals' life" (Creswll, 2005, p. 8). In addition, it also enables me to consider "the specific contexts in which people live and work to achieve an awareness of [their] historical and cultural settings" (Creswll, 2005, p. 8) through a conscious study of rhetorical symbols and their potential impact on the individuals' reactions.

2.4 Why Comparative Rhetorical Approach

The project conducts a comparative study of rhetorical and cultural influences on U.S. and Chinese approaches to global copyright practice. It studies rhetorical traditions that have existed and are existing in different societies (Kennedy, 1998, p. 1).This approach is based on the assumption that rhetorical practice is universal but culturally unique. It aims at identifying the similarities and differences practiced by separate cultures, and applying the knowledge learned from this comparison and contrast in cross-cultural communication.

The comparative approach is nothing new in the field of social sciences. It has always existed as an essential tool for generating knowledge (Ghorra-Gobin, 2003) by "reveal[ing] features of some object of study that may not be immediately evident in its own context" (Kennedy, 1998, p. 1). Researchers in many disciplines have used a comparative approach. For example, anthropologist Edward T. Hall (1976) applied this method in his investigation of the mode of human communication between cultures. He found that some cultures tend to depend on context more than others in interpersonal communication and thus developed the concept of high- and low-context orientations to distinguish differences in communication. Hall identified the characteristics of high-context communication as being less explicit, relying more on internalized understanding, and encouraging long-term relationships while low-context cultures tend to be more explicit in human interactions, are more rule- and task-oriented, and short duration of interpersonal connections.

Robert Oliver's (1971) groundbreaking investigation in the book of *Communication and Culture in Ancient India and China* was not a typical comparison between Western and Eastern communication, as he mainly focused on two Eastern cultures. However, he certainly broadened the scope of Western communication research with a fresher perspective of communication in China and India in ancient times.

George Kennedy (1998), a pioneer in our field, attempted a cross-cultural rhetorical study. He offered a comparative overview of rhetoric as a universal human practice of communication in his work of *Comparative Rhetoric: An Historical and Cross-Cultural Introduction*. As modest as he was to claim that his effort was only to entail more mature study, he examined many cultures such as the South Pacific, Africa, the Americas, as well as the Near East, China, India, Greece, and Rome. He addressed commonalities in all rhetorical traditions and differences in individual cultures. Following in his footsteps, Lu (1998) surveyed ancient Chinese rhetoric, utilizing Greek rhetoric as a reference (p. 13). Steven Combs approached comparative rhetoric more methodologically. He identified the Daoist rhetoric as a method of rhetorical criticism and applied it in his critique of four U.S. movies: *The Tao of Steve, A Bug's Life, Antz,* and *Shrek* to illustrate the differences between Western and Daoist values, which offered an alternative lens in addition to Western rhetorical theory (2006).

Rhetorical practice is universal. Kennedy (1998) demonstrated that all ancient cultures presented rhetoric as a mental or emotional energy that had been employed to preserve the best interest of the rhetor on both individual and community levels. When classical Greek rhetoric flourished in the fifth century B. C. E., Chinese intellectuals were also practicing persuasion to rulers of the kingdoms and social elites. Interestingly enough, although Greece and China never influenced each other's rhetorical experience, they both recognized rhetoric's function in persuasion. They both associated rhetorical practice with many disciplines such as politics, law, and ethics to test and convey knowledge. Therefore, we can generalize that language, culture, and rhetoric are intertwined to shape what humans perceive the world and how we interact with the environment surrounding us.

Rhetoric is also culturally bound, meaning that each rhetorical tradition is endowed with a uniqueness particular of that culture. This is because rhetorical tradition is situated in a cultural context with a distinctive political, socio-economic, and cultural environment. Kennedy (1998) and many other rhetoricians identified the universal function of rhetoric (Bizzell and Herzberg, 2001). They also acknowledged different characteristics of rhetorics practiced by cultures in various ways (Oliver, 1971; Kennedy, 1998; Lu, 1998). These cultural characteristics are destined to influence individuals with different perspectives and in their unique ways as will be briefly depicted later in this chapter.

Given the universality and uniqueness of each rhetorical tradition, Kennedy proposed the following objectives for the study of comparative rhetoric (1998, *Preface*):

- Identify universality and distinctiveness of rhetorical traditions.
- Formulate general questions that might apply to any

rhetorical traditions.
- Form structures and text terminologies that different rhetorical practices share, and apply the knowledge we have learned in the field of rhetoric to cross-cultural communication.

My project combines the first and the last objective, responding particularly to Kennedy's call to comparing and contrasting what the U.S. and Chinese rhetorical traditions share or differ. Then it applies the knowledge learned in the comparison and contrast to the understanding of cultural values and beliefs associated with U.S.-China conflict over global copyright practice in China.

For the rhetorical comparison, the project first adopts the method of cluster analysis to examine the concept of *virtue/ethos* both Greek/Roman and Chinese rhetorical traditions share and key terms clustering the concept which are relevant to ideas of law, social order, individual obligations and rights. I also compare and contrast their similarities and differences between how the two traditions perceived the concept to explore possible connections between these key terms and legal/copyright awareness in the two cultures.

2.5 Cluster Analysis: An Approach to Articulate the Author's Intention on the Audience

Cluster analysis, developed by Kenneth Burke, identifies and examines the meanings, connections, and implications of clustering terms. In this method, "key terms that appear often in the artifact or are of high intensity are selected for analysis" (Nowlen et. al. in Foss, 2004, p. 102). Burke established this method on the basis that men are "symbol-using, symbol-making, and symbol-misusing animals" (1966, p. 6) who construct meanings from their motivation of symbolicity (p. 6) and link the writer, the audience, and the context. Burke believed that rhetoric, through human language use, aims "to form attitudes or to induce actions in other human agents" (1969, p. 41): symbols are "parallel to a pattern of experience" (1933, p. 14), and the using of which induces cooperation in beings that by nature respond to symbols (p. 16).

Burke used identification to describe the relationship between language and actions the rhetor aims (consciously or unconsciously) to prompt from the audience. He employed this term synonymously with consubstantiality, meaning shared substance or interests that "constitutes an identification between an individual and some property or person" (Foss, 2004, p. 70): "To identify A with B is to make A 'consubstantial' with B" (1968, p. 20). The concept of identification does not stand alone. According to Burke, it is "compensatory to division" (1968, p. 22) because "individuals are [constantly] at odds with one another, or become identified with groups more or less at odds with one another" (1968, p. 22). The conflict calls for "a need for the rhetorician to proclaim their unity" (1968, p. 22) by naming or defining the situation for the audience (Foss, 2004, p. 70). Therefore, rhetoric preserves or changes social order by influencing the way individuals perceive their symbolic relations. It is rooted in language use in a historical sense, but it is embedded in all human actions where meanings could be found: where there is meaning, there is persuasion; where there is human action, there is rhetoric.

Rhetoric also presents instructions or solutions to a problem to assist its audience in different ways:

> It may provide a vocabulary of thoughts, actions, emotions and attitudes for codifying and thus interpreting a situation. It may encourage the acceptance of a situation that cannot be changed, or it may serve as a guide for how to correct a situation... It may help rhetors justify their conduct, turning actions that seem to be ethical or absurd into ones considered virtuous or accurate (Foss, 2004, p. 70).

Rhetoric's basic functions, as Foss summarized from Burke in his *Counter-Statement* (p. 153-157), indicate that rhetors, in using words, form attitudes or actions in other human agents (Bizzell and Herzberg, 2001, p. 1337). Rhetoric creates the terministic screens through which rhetors (as well as all other human agents) select to describe the world that directs our attention to particular aspects of reality rather than others (Foss, 2004, p. 71). Burke further claimed that "Even if any given terminology is a reflection of reality, by its very nature as a terminology it must be a selection of reality; and to this extent it must function also as a deflection of reality" (1968, p. 45).

The dichotomy of selection/deflection allows the rhetorical critic to "gain insights into rhetors by analyzing the terministic screens evidenced in their rhetoric" (Foss, 2004, p. 71). More importantly, it examines the "implications of the particular terminology in terms of which the observations are made" (1968, p. 46, originally italicized by Burke) because "much of that we take as observations about 'reality' may be but the spinning out of possibilities implicit in our particular choices of terms" (1968, p. 46). The notions of identification and terministic screens are significant for my project because when I critique early Western and Chinese texts, I can examine in what direction ancient rhetors were leading their audience through emphasizing these key terms. I can also explore their implicit meanings that may or may not be known to the rhetors themselves, but are significant for the readers/audiences.

Table 2. 1: Western/Greco-Roman and Chinese Texts and Key Terms

Western/Chinese Texts	Key Terms/Virtue or Ethos
Protagoras	virtue, knowledge, unity of virtue (wisdom, justice, temperance, holiness, and courage), and justice
On Rhetoric	ethos (practical wisdom, virtue, goodwill), justice
De Oratore	ideal orator, universal knowledge, knowledge of public law
The Analects	ren/benevolence, li/ritual, zheng ming/rectification of names, cardinal relationships
Mencius	ren/Benevolence, li/ritual, benevolent governance
Dao De Jing	dao/the Way, wu wei/inaction, bu zheng/non-contention

To integrate cluster analysis in my study, I first identify key terms of human virtuousness. Both Western and Chinese rhetoricians agreed upon rhetoric's function in molding individuals and society. They emphasized that *virtue* led to democratic, ideal, just, and equal or harmonious societies and thus, advocated adamantly to instill it in the mind of their audience. I then emphasize terms closely associated with the key terms (See Table 2. 1. above) that may support, explain, complement, or are the means by which human virtue could be established.

In sum, Burke's critical approaches provides me the opportunity to discover a rhetor's worldviews through the investigation of rhetoric that constitutes identification, terministic screens, and many other notions (Foss, 2004, p. 71). The method also offers me the opportunity to examine the meanings of clustering symbols based on their frequency and intensity in the surveyed texts. In other words, cluster criticism helps the critic to discover the interrelationships among these equations that the rhetor may not be conscious of but are meaningful for the audience. When I adopt this method to my project, I attempt to interpret what these rhetoricians intended for or expected of their audience and critique their potential connection with legal/copyright awareness and practice.

2.6 Intercultural Rhetoric/Communication: The Approach to Cultural Values and Beliefs as Well as Behaviors

Intercultural rhetoric/communication compares values, behaviors, institutions and organizations (Hofstede, 2001), and represents a neighboring discipline to the discourse of rhetoric. Given that it examines how people of different cultures view the world and act accordingly, researchers have recognized the association of rhetorical practice and cultural orientations, acknowledging the influence of rhetorical traditions on a culture's thinking pattern, decision-making, consequent behaviors (Foss, 2004; Golden, Berquist, and Coleman, 1983; Kennedy, 1998; Lu, 1998; Combs, 2006), as well as the reflection of the latter in rhetorical traditions. Scholars in a variety of disciplines have examined many cultural dimensions in human communication across cultures (Triandis, 1994; Hall, 1976; Hofstede, 2001; Hampden-Turner and Trompenaars, 2000). I find the following three cultural dimensions especially relevant to my study. This is because they present features particular of the target cultures with respect to such notions as rule of law, individualism, group interest, equality, ownership, freedom, liberty, etc. connected with copyright practice. These dimensions are:

- Universalism versus particularism
- Individualism versus collectivism/communitarianism
- Low- versus high-power distance

Universalism and particularism are value standards that may guide human behavior at individual and national levels (Hampden-Turner and Trompenaars, 2000). All cultures carry these dichotomous orientations, but a culture may tend to lean more towards one than the other. For example, a universalistic culture relies on common values, searching for "sameness and similarity" and "tries to impose on all members of a class or universe the laws of their commonality" (Hampden-Turner and Trompenaars, 2000, p. 14). Thus, universalistic societies more likely try to put everything under the control of general rules, indicating that law is especially important in organizing society. This cultural trend is manifest in the consistent effort to globalize intellectual property rights (IPR) protection on the part of the U.S., copyright included, in developing countries. Therefore, the U.S. represents a typical universalistic based on the following criteria (Hampden-Turner and Trompenaars, 2000, p. 17):

- Common belief in natural right for humans and rules of law
- Shared allegiance to the country by people of diverse ethnicity
- Appreciation of science, discovery, and methodologies of inquiry
- Cherish of economic and military power, globalization, mass manufacturing and mass marketing

On the contrary, particularism embraces "exceptions, circumstances, and relations" (Hampden-Turner and Trompenaars, 2000, p. 13; Nawojczy, 2006, p. 3062) and allows particular phenomena to come before general rules. This cultural trend easily encounters clashes with any external pressure that intends to force upon it universal rules, such as global IP/copyright practice. Particularistic cultures may apply laws based on the social standing of the persons involved (Thatcher, 2000). China is a particularistic culture based on its trust in relationships, acceptance of exceptions associated with "what is unique and incomparable about people, situation, and event", use of power and coercion rather than legality, allegiance to super-naturalism as ethnic identity (Hampden-Turner and Trompenaars, 2000, p. 22, 24).

The second dimension of cultural variability is individualism as opposed to collectivism (communitarianism). It "describes the relationship between the individual with the collectivity that prevails in a given society" (Hofstede, 2001, p. 209). As reflected in its values and beliefs, an individualist culture celebrates "competition, self-reliance, self-interest, and personal growth and fulfillment" while a collectivist culture values "more important cooperation, social concern, altruism, public service and social legacy" (Hampden-Turner and Trompenaars, 2000, p. 68). This is to say that an individualist culture tends to be more self-oriented and a collectivist culture focuses more on the in-group interest. Hofstede reported the U.S. ranks the most individualist culture among the 50 countries he surveyed. He reached the conclusion based on the criteria of "'I' consciousness, self-orientation, universal standard, emphasis on individual initiative and achievement, right to private life, modern or postmodern society" (2001, p. 227).

Collectivism/communitarianism "encourages members [of the group] to leave a legacy to society, neighborhood, and family, which lasts beyond the individual life" (Hampden-Turner and Trompenaars, 2000, p. 79). This is to say that people on the collectivist side are integrated, from birth on, into extended in-groups that prioritize collective and inner group interests over individual ones (Hofstede, 2001). China is the lowest individualist country among the countries investigated–showing the characteristics of "'we' consciousness, collective orientation, particularist, membership ideal, less consciousness of private life, activities imposed by context, traditional society" (Hofstede, 2001, p. 227). For instance, for a long time in China, a formal copyright law was entirely missing in the legal discourse. Authors were not benefited much from their creations because copyrights belonged to the nation. In return for their work, they received a very small manuscript fee.

Power distance, the last cultural dimension to be discussed in this chapter, refers to the extent to which a society accepts human inequality (Hofstede, 2001, p. 79). According to Hofstede (2001), human inequality in a society is multidimensional and can occur in various areas, such as "physical and mental characteristics, social status and prestige, wealth, power, laws, rights, and rules" (p. 80). Cultures scoring low on power distance index (PDI) tend to view hierarchy as inequality. Low power distance cultures consider all people have equal rights and should be received for what they have achieved rather than ascribed (Hampden-Turner and Trompenaars, 2000). On the other hand, cultures scoring high on PDI privilege hierarchy, accepting that the more powerful are superior to the less powerful, and believing that human inequality is normal and helps maintain societal order (Hofstede, 2001).

The United States represents a low PDI country. Scoring 40 in Hofstede's survey, it pursues equal rights, adheres to power balance and check, and prioritizes achievement and a level playing field. It also values empiricism, pragmatism, and utilitarianism. Contrarily, China scores 80 in the survey, indicating a high inequality of power and wealth distribution. The power difference reflects each culture's legal approach. The U.S. may grant equal treatment to individuals while China may favor the privileged.

Now, to apply the method of intercultural rhetoric/communication to my study and explore the meanings of cultural values and beliefs as well as implications in each culture's approach to legal and copyright practice, I first identify and interpret major cultural values and beliefs from selected texts and present their significances in their respective cultural contexts. Then, drawing basic cultural features as my criteria, I present the findings. Lastly, I compare and contrast American and Chinese cultural dimensions and their potential impact on copyright practice.

In sum, the approach of intercultural rhetoric/communication emphasizes values and beliefs significant in different cultures to decipher how individuals of a particular culture understand and approach the world surrounding them. In other words, cultural values and beliefs shape our thinking orientations and influence how we behave. When I interpret and critique values and beliefs reflected in the texts, I intend to understand what these values and beliefs are, what they mean, if they exemplify the cultural dimensions researchers have identified, and how they might affect the U.S. and Chinese in their view of formal laws and copyright practice.

2.7 Marxist Criticism: An Ideological Approach to the U.S.-China Conflicts over Copyright Practice

The ideological approach in rhetorical criticism is also a relevant lens in this project. As suggested by the term itself, ideological criticism deals with ideologies, beliefs and values that reflect a group's fundamental political, economic, social, and cultural interests. The U.S.-China conflicts that involve the U.S. promotion of copyright practice in China and the Chinese response to the effort exemplify an ideological encounter.

While emerging from a number of social and political perspectives ranging from structuralism, semiotics/semiology, feminism, and others, Marxism has a tremendous impact on ideological criticism. The key concepts, such as base/superstructure, hegemony, and ideological practice provide a critical and crucial lens through which ideological criticism examines ideologies that are either dominant or embedded in artifacts (Foss, 2004, p.243). Central in the approach is the claim that ideologies or different patterns of beliefs and values exist in any culture and are manifest in rhetorical artifacts. Classical Marxism stated that ideology is demonstrated in the way a society organizes its means of economic production and consequently, some groups possess dominant positions politically, economically, and socially over the others (Marx and Engels in Storey, 2001, p.3). Accordingly, it argued that rhetorical texts and practices must be analyzed and understood in their historical contexts of production (Storey, 1998, p. 187).

In addition, neo-Marxism in modern times broadens the scope of ideological criticism. For instance, the theory of hegemony developed by Italian theorist Antonio Gramsci asserts that economic production is "a condition in process in which a dominant class...does not merely rule a society but leads it through the exercise of 'moral and intellectual leadership'"(Storey, 2001, p. 103). By this, Gramsci meant that the ideas of the ruling class are not passively imposed upon the subordinate; rather, they are negotiated and modified through making concessions and sharing interests (Hall, 2001, p. 77; Edger & Sedgwick, 1999).

Using Marxism as an analytical tool, I first contextualize the U.S.-China copyright conflict by briefly introducing the development of copyright protection in the world. I divide the development into two stages of internationalization and globalization which are represented respectively by the *Berne Convention* and the *TRIPS Agreement*. The development offers the historical context against which the U.S.-China conflicts arose and were settled as indicated in the *Memorandum of Understanding* in 1992 (the *1992 MOU*) and the *Intellectual Property Rights Agreement* (the *1995 IP Agreement*). The two agreements illustrate the results of domination, coercion, concessions, and negotiations that exemplify the effort of copyright/intellectual property rights internationalization and globalization and provide major elements Marxist approach (classical and neo-Gramsci) studies.

Following the introduction of the development of copyright practice in the world, the discussion moves to the *1992 MOU*. First, it presents a brief background of the conflict and a summary of the *MOU*. Then, the discussion focuses on Article 3 which is solely concerned with copyright protection and describes each clause, paying special attention to the content, such as the parties' separate and mutual duties for a better understanding of the relationships formed from the agreement and the implications embodied.

The *1995 IP Agreement* complements the *1992 MOU* by stressing protection of intellectual property rights that the *MOU* lacks. The Agreement Letter highlights China's effort to improve intellectual property rights protection through judicial, administrative procedures as well as enforcement actions while the Action Plan details the enforcement structure, information dissemination, and education and public campaigns. The efforts and actions plans are intertwined with the protection of all three major types of intellectual property rights. However, my examination of the Action Plan underscores the protection of copyright.

Document analysis using Marxist criticism falls into three major parts: the development of copyright protection in the world and the U.S.-China copyright conflict. The first part briefly describes internationalization and globalization of world copyright practice and contextualizes the second part by portraying the process and standard setting of two world copyright treatises. The second part focuses on the U. S.-China conflicts happened in early 1990s settled by the *1992*

MOU and the *1995 IP Agreement*. It pays special attention to obligations of the two sides with respect to copyright protection. The last part will be a comparison of ideological orientations of the U.S.-China and their potential impact on copyright practice.

2.8 Researcher Role

Rhetorical criticism offers the inquirer an opportunity to investigate and explain symbolic acts and artifacts for the purpose of understanding rhetorical process (Foss, 2004, p. 6). The project allows me to declare two positions. The first is that of a graduate student of rhetoric and professional communication who believes she has the responsibilities to explore rhetorical practice and its impact on communication. Having pursued doctoral studies with a special academic interest in rhetorical practices of different cultures, I make the assumption that my research will contribute to the corpus of knowledge for and about rhetorical traditions and their influence on cross-cultural communication.

The second position in which I situate myself is the privilege as a Chinese student with access to higher education both in China and the United States. I am motivated to choose the topic of the U.S.-China copyright debate which is considered one of the top U.S.-China business issues and thus, important and meaningful to study.

My education and training in rhetoric, as well as my ability to speak both languages presents a privilege. This privilege makes it possible for me to cross borders and access the insider knowledge concerning the rhetorical, cultural, and ideological factors that contribute to the two cultures' copyright approaches. However, I recognize that this insider knowledge may still cause concerns about neutrality within academics due to the limitations of access to as much information/research in Chinese as in English as well as using Western perspectives (comparative rhetoric, intercultural rhetoric/communication, and Marxist method) in a study involving China. My response to the concern is that I share every step of the research process to present the findings as accurately as possible.

2. 9   Research Materials

As I mentioned earlier, rhetorical criticism engages in a systematic investigation and explanation of symbolic acts and artifacts that are "enduring" and whose "importance and functions" are "immediate and ephemeral" (Foss, 2004, p. 7). In order to examine *the ways rhetorical and cultural traditions in the U.S. and China impact understanding and enforcement of copyright in their respective countries and ways the implications are influential in U.S.-China professional communication,* I have chosen three sets of texts to represent Western and Chinese rhetorical traditions, the U.S. and China's cultural values and beliefs, and ideologies reflected and impacted copyright approaches of the U.S. and China.

2.9.1 Set One: Early Greco-Roman and Chinese Texts

The first set of texts includes three Western and three Chinese canonical classics:

- *Protagoras* by Plato
- *On Rhetoric* by Aristotle
- *De Oratore* by Cicero
- *The Analects* by Confucius
- *Mencius* by Mencius
- *Dao De Jing* by Lao Zi

The Western texts stress the concepts of *virtue/ethos, justice, knowledge,* and *knowledge of public law.* The Chinese texts indicate that ancient Chinese viewed human virtuousness differently. The Confucians believed *ren* (benevolence, love, gentility, etc.) is the highest human virtue, asserting that if everybody cultivated virtual character, society would be consequently in order. They suggested following the Zhou *li*, rituals and norms of the previous Dynasty that enjoyed prosperity and social harmony and offered benevolent governance. The Daoists represented by Lao Zi in his *Dao De Jing* rejected human intrusion and believed observing the natural flow of Nature, the *Dao* without contention would be the real human *virtue.* Both Western and Chinese rhetoricians believed that the concept of *virtue* shapes an individual as a person and influences societal order as a whole and therefore, I consider the concept relevant to my topic.

The concept of *virtue/ethos* is relevant to the project because it indicates normative perspectives and is instrumental on "why people follow the law and the extent to which normative factors influence compliance with the law" (Tyler, 2006). *Virtue/ethos* still impacts how people of [even] modern times behave toward laws. If people view compliance with the law as appropriate, they will voluntarily assume the obligation to follow legal rules (Tyler, 2006, p. 3). That is, individuals who have virtual qualities are more willing to abide by the law which consequently, makes law enforcement more effective. The selection of the first set of texts is based on this perspective of the concept of *virtue/ethos*. I locate terms that highlight the concept and explore their meanings and implications regarding to formal legal practice that includes copyright protection (See Table 2. 1). Now, the following discussion provides an introduction to each separate artifact starting from Greek rhetoric.

Rhetoric in Western history has been an important and separate discipline to be learned in the classroom, practiced in the court and at public assemblies, and conceptualized by rhetoricians in their speeches and writings. The moral concept associated with Western and U.S. approach to legal practice, copyright included, such as the view of *virtue/ethos*, knowledge, and *justice* is found in the lengthy and profound discussions of rhetorical works by Plato, Aristotle, and Cicero.

In *Protagoras*, Plato talked about *virtue* throughout the dialogue. Explaining the unity of *virtue* (*justice, temperance, holiness, courage,* and *wisdom*), he stressed that each type of *virtue* was *knowledge* and especially the importance of *justice* in terms of social order. These terms represent the ideal of an individual orator engaging in rhetorical practice intended to make better persons and bring good to the society as a whole.

Aristotle uttered as explicitly as Plato the significant role *virtue* played in oratory, emphasizing it as a major element of *ethos* for the speaker to establish himself worthy of credence in persuasion. He viewed *ethos* as a component of rhetorical argument and thus an artistic achievement for the effective speaker. Therefore, in *On Rhetoric, ethos* will be the key term. *Virtue* and *justice* that cluster around *ethos* will also be examined in terms of their meanings, significance, implications, and association with my study. Chapters 2, 4, 5, 9, and 13 of Book One and Chapter 1 of Book Two of *On Rhetoric* are the main focus where *ethos, virtue,* and *justice* are mostly discussed.

Cicero's concept of *virtue* focused on the quality of an *ideal orator* which is the key term in *De Oratore*. Cicero pointed out that an *ideal orator* should be an expert of his topics and be equipped with *universal knowledge*. In particular, he should have the *knowledge of public law* which was significant in different rhetorical contexts, especially in the court where *justice* and injustice were involved. Sections I, VI, VIII, XI, and XLVI of Book One, will be the focus.

Early Chinese rhetorical practice embedded its moral concepts in the works of politics, ethics, and philosophy. Therefore, *The Analects* which records Confucius' sayings becomes the first choice of early Chinese text for the project due to its significance in ancient Chinese philosophy, politics, ethics, education, art, and rhetoric. The terms particularly relevant to *virtue/ethos* are *ren* (benevolence) and *li* (rituals). *Zheng ming* (rectifying of names) and *cardinal relationships* are two important concepts surrounding *ren* and *li*. These notions demonstrate Confucius' perception of individuals' moral cultivation, duties, and societal harmonization. The examination of these terms focuses on Chapters I, II, IV, VI, VII, XII, XIII, and XVI where there are ample examples and explanations.

Mencius continued Confucius' legacy. However, he stressed that persuasion should be focused on educating rulers for *benevolent governance* and good citizens in the state. Unlike Confucius who regarded rulers highly, Mencius argued that rulers ought to be dethroned by their subjects if they failed to rule the state with *justice* and *benevolence*. Consequently, *ren* continues to be the key terms while *li* and *benevolent governance* are associated terms and the focus of Mencius' concept of *virtue* will emphasize Chapters I, II, IV, VI, VII, XXXII.

If *The Analects* was intended mainly for the rulers and social elites and *Mencius* enhanced the Confucian notion of *ren* with *benevolent governance*, Lao Zi's *Dao De Jing* is the only book among the three that provides practical wisdom for the general public. The major theme related to this topic is *dao*, the Way of nature surrounded by terms of *de* (*virtue*), *wu wei* (in-action) and *bu zheng* (non-contention) that Lao Zi stressed as means of individual moral cultivation and social harmony. Therefore, the analysis of the documents of *Dao De Jing* will concentrate on Chapters I, VI, VIII, X, XVIII, LI, XXVIII, XXXVII, and LXXX where Lao Zi has discussed these concepts.

2.9.2 Set Two: U.S. and Later Chinese Texts

Based on their political, rhetorical, cultural, and legal significance, the following four U.S. and later Chinese texts are selected as the second set of data for the project:

- *The Constitutions of the United States of America* (the *U.S. Constitution*)
- *The Declaration of Independence* (the *Declaration*)
- *The Constitution of the People's Republic of China* (*China's Constitution*)
- *Deng Xiaoping's Southern Tour Speeches* (*Deng's Speeches*)

In addition, cultural dimensions of universalism/particularism, individualism/collectivism (communitarianism), and low and high power distance are the primary theoretical underpinnings in analyzing these texts.

The significance of these texts is obvious. The *Declaration of Independence* justified the revolt against a government which no longer guaranteed the interests of the governed. It also stated certain ideals which became U.S. cultural values and beliefs, such as independence, freedom, equality, and individual rights. The constitutions are supreme laws of the two countries and function as the basis and source of legal authority underlying the existence of the two countries and their governments. In addition, they are mirror images of the two countries' beliefs and values and legal culture. *Deng's Speeches* are not legal documents, but they convinced China to continue its economic reform efforts which impact Chinese life in every way.

The intimate association between rhetorical traditions and cultural values and beliefs validate the application of cultural variability. As I have described at the beginning of the chapter, rhetorical traditions shape a culture's beliefs and values that certainly include perceptions of copyright practice. For instance, the concepts of freedom, democracy, and equality, when reflected in copyright practice, will equate more public awareness of the legal rights of copyright holders and enforcement by the government. Contrarily, if peace, harmony, and development of the entire society become priorities, individual copyright holders may face more losses when rampant piracy occurs and power abuse hinders effective copyright enforcement.

The analysis of the U.S. texts starts with the *Declaration of Independence*, focusing mainly on cultural values and beliefs evident in the document, such as independence, freedom, equality, and democracy that have shaped the essence of the *U.S. Constitution* and culture. Then, the analysis moves to the *U.S. Constitution*. First, I examine the preamble and discuss briefly some of the sections in Article One and Two about powers of and limitations on government branches. Next, I concentrate on the Bill of Rights that deals with fundamental rights of individuals that are related to the assumptions of copyright. Universal rules (universalism), "I" focus (individualism), and equal rights and opportunity for individuals (low power distance) will be my criteria to evaluate cultural values and beliefs.

The analysis of the *Constitution of the People's Republic of China* focuses on the sections relevant to the project: the Preamble, Articles 1, 3, 6, 8, 10, 13, 20, 24, 28 in Chapter One of the Guidelines, and Chapter Two of the Fundamental Rights and Duties of Citizens. The Preamble introduces the contemporary history of China and praises highly the Communist Party, indicating China's political preference. The nine articles in the Guidelines define China's political entity, identify its economic systems, and present Chinese government's approach to science, technology, morality, and patriotism. The study of *Deng Xiaoping's Southern Tour Speeches* emphasizes the first speech Deng delivered in the City of Shenzhen, Guangdong Province where China started its first experiment of market economy in 1984. Socialism with Chinese characteristics, state and collective ownerships, collectivism, patriotism, etc. are typical Chinese cultural values and beliefs in the two texts. I use exceptions (particularism), "we" focus, and hierarchy as standards to evaluate and categorize the cultural values and beliefs.

Following the interpretation of the U.S. and Chinese texts, the analysis compares and contrasts cultural dimensions of each culture and their potential implications for legal and copyright approach.

2.9.3   Set Three: Chinese and U.S. Copyright-Related Texts

This part of the project stresses two bilateral intellectual property right treatises which are the results of the U.S.-China copyright conflicts in the 1990s and illustrates the two countries' relationship with respect to copyright practice:

- *Memorandum of Understanding between the Government of United States and the Government of the People's Republic of China on the Protection of Intellectual Property 1992* (*The 1992 MOU*)
- *The U.S.-China Intellectual Property Rights Agreement 1995* (*The 1995 IP Agreement*).

The purposes of this examination are twofold: portraying the ideological encounter of global copyright promotion and exploring copyright approach of the U.S. and China. I first provide a brief introduction of the internationalization and globalization of world copyright promotion to set up the historical context, paying special attention to their standard setting and major content regarding copyright protection. Then I study the treatises, also focusing on the content about copyright protection. Lastly, I compare and contrast the two cultures' copyright approach reflected in the conflict.

2.10 Conclusion

In this chapter, I reviewed methods and artifacts to be used in the research. The next three chapters will present findings of the researched texts. In Chapter Three, I apply the method of cluster analysis to explore earlier Greek/Roman and Chinese concept of *virtue/ethos* and compare and contrast its implications for legal (copyright) practice in separate cultures. In Chapter Four, I examine the U.S. and Chinese texts, locate major cultural values and beliefs, explore their meanings, and compare and contrast their significance in shaping the two cultures' copyright approach. Three cultural dimensions will be the method in the study. Chapter Five emphasizes a Marxist approach to the U.S.-China copyright conflicts in the early 1990s. Two bilateral treaties regarding copyright practice in China will be studied in the context of world copyright internationalization and globalization.

Chapter Three
Rhetorical Tradtions and Western (U.S.)/ Chinese Legal (Copyright) Approaches —A Cluster Analysis

3.1 Introduction

This chapter, the first of three data analysis chapters, addresses Western (U.S.) and Chinese rhetorical traditions and their possible influence on how the two cultures approach legal (copyright) practice by applying the method of cluster analysis. I place the word legal here and copyright in the parenthesis because the concept of copyright did not exist in ancient times. However, I believe a culture's legal tradition impacts its approach to copyright practiced in modern times. As mentioned in previous chapters, both cultures enjoy a rich rhetorical heritage that informs, influences, and shapes their people on how they view the world and communicate with the context in which they live. While the U.S. carries the Greco-Roman rhetorical tradition and has enhanced and adapted it to the particular U.S. context, China's rhetorical tradition has continued to permeate in the Chinese culture for over two thousand years.

In the process of data analysis, to understand the association between rhetorical traditions and legal (copyright) approach, I focus on the key rhetorical notions roughly grouped in the category of *virtue/ethos* that suggest a strong connection with legal practice in both Western and Chinese rhetorical classics. In other words, analysis of the texts in this chapter aims to answer the question of "How do rhetors use the concept of *virtue/ethos* and other clustering terms to persuade their audiences to adhere to the prescribed beliefs and values associated with formal legal practice (such as copyright)?" In the following discussion, I present the meanings of this notion and other related terms in their particular cultural context and compare and contrast their implications for Western and Chinese copyright approaches.

3.2 Rule by Law or Rule by Man: the Concept of *Virtue/Ethos* in Early Greco/Roman and Chinese Rhetorical Traditions

Both ancient Western and Chinese philosophers and rhetoricians held that an individual's sense of *virtue/ethos* played an important role in his attitude toward and conduct in the context he lived and thus, constituted an integral part in maintaining societal order (*Protagoras, On Rhetoric, The Analects*, etc.). The concept of *virtue/ethos* has a broad scope in Western and Chinese rhetoric. It includes *virtue, justice, temperance, holiness, courage* (*Protagoras*); *practical wisdom, virtue, goodwill* (*On Rhetoric*); and *knowledge* (*De Oratore*). It is also *benevolence, ritual, benevolent governance* (*The Analects and Mencius*) and the *Way* and *virtue* (*Dao De Jing*). Regardless of the wide scope, both Western and Chinese ancient rhetoric viewed *virtue/ethos* as human moral characters that shape individuals and influence society. However, they obviously interpreted the concept differently. For the purpose of my analysis, I use *virtue/ethos* as the macro-category that encloses other sub-categories (See Table 2. 1.). I argue that the idea of *virtue/ethos* is culturally situated and may contribute to how the Western/U.S. and Chinese approach to formal laws such as copyright. A cluster analysis of the notions helps support this point.

In the rest of this chapter, I first focus on the Greek and Roman texts: *Protagoras, On Rhetoric,* and *De Oratore* by providing a brief introduction of each of them. Next, I identify the terms of *virtue/ethos* and other related elements and interpret their meanings. Then, I discuss the Chinese texts in the similar manner. In the end, I compare and contrast these concepts in their separate cultural contexts in relation to their potential impact on such formal legal practice as copyright.

3.3 Plato's Concept of *Virtue* in *Protagoras*

Protagoras is one of a number of supremely important early Socratic dialogues by Plato (428 B.C.E.-347 B.C.E.) who was characterized as a prominent Greek philosopher that held such seminal aspirations of his works as to plant seeds of *knowledge* in young minds and was widely acknowledged to have fulfilled his expectation by his eminent position in the history of Western thought (Bizzell and Herzberg, 2001, p. 28). In *Protagoras,* Plato adopted a dialectic method in his argument through Socrates and debated with the great sophist Protagoras over two major themes: the teachability of *virtue* and *virtue* as *knowledge*. Plato's goal was to refute Protagoras' claim that he, as one of the infamous sophists, was professing *knowledge* to his students.

The first section of the dialogue emphasizes the argument between Socrates and Protagoras over the teachability of *virtue*. Socrates maintained that *virtue* was not *knowledge* (*Protagoras,* 312-328), and therefore, could not be taught. The other section focuses on Socrates' effort to prove that all the *virtues* are connected with a single kind of *knowledge* (Nehamas, 1990, p. 3), the mastery of which guarantees the individuals to behave virtuously or otherwise. This conflict illustrates Plato's paradoxical doctrine of the nature of *virtue* and suffices to indicate Plato's endorsement of Protagoras' point of view toward *virtue* which is teachable *knowledge*.

My study explores Plato's *virtue*. It also stresses the clustering terms of *knowledge*, the unity of *virtue*, and *justice* which are human moral qualities (See table 3.1) due to their relatedness to the public's sense of legal practice.

Table 3. 1 Western/Greco-Roman and Chinese Key Notions of Virtue and Surrounding Terms

Concepts of Virtue	Surrounding Terms
Plato/virtue	knowledge, unity of virtue, justice
Aristotle/ethos	practical wisdom, unity of virtue, goodwill, justice
Ideal orator	universal knowledge, knowledge of public law
Confucius/*ren*	*li, zheng ming*, cardinal relationships
Mencius/*ren*	*ren* governance
Lao Zi/*Dao*	*de, wu wei, bu zheng*

3.3.1 How Virtue Shapes the Person

In *Protagoras*, the teachability of *virtue*, *virtue* as *knowledge* and *virtue* as *a unity* are the central themes in the argument between Socrates and Protagoras. The term *virtue* appears more than forty times in the dialogue. It makes its first appearance when Protagoras claims that he teaches his students *virtue,* and equates it to "the prudence in affairs private as well as public" (*Protagoras,* 318, p. 12). Protagoras was confident that his students would learn to "order [their] own house in the best manner, and ...speak and act for the best in the affairs of the state" (*Protagoras,* 318, p. 12). Plato first called this type of teaching "the art of politics" (*Protagoras,* 319-320, pp. 12-13) and "the knowledge of the soul" (*Protagoras,* 313, p. 8), and later *virtue* throughout the dialogue. Although Plato had reservations about the teachability of *virtue* at the beginning, he never questioned the significance and function of *virtue* in shaping an individual as a person and a citizen. He later consented that individuals could develop and cultivate their sense of *virtue* through constant education and experience.

3.3.2 Virtue Is Knowledge

Plato substituted *knowledge* for *virtue* and divided it into two types: expert and non-expert *knowledge*, and considered *virtue* the foundation of human good decisions. Expert and specialized *knowledge* was connected with ordinary skills, such as shipbuilding, carpentry, and flute-playing (*Protagoras,* 319, p.13) and less specialized *knowledge* was human *knowledge* and related to *virtue* (Everson, 1990, p. 66). With expert *knowledge*, Plato provided professional criteria, but none for non-expert *knowledge/virtue* (Everson, 1990, p. 67). For instance, a carpenter should know carpentry and a ship builder must know how to build a ship, There were not specific criteria for *virtue* since anybody (timbers, cobblers, sailors, passengers, rich and poor, high and low) without formal training in political art could participate in politics and wise men did not teach their sons to be virtuous persons (*Protagoras,* 319-320, pp. 12-13). However, when Socrates stopped questioning about the teachability of *virtue,* he agreed with Protagoras that *virtue* is *knowledge* and can be acquired and taught (*Protagoras,* 324, p. 17).

Virtue as *knowledge* influences human decisions. Plato once asserted that "the erring act" of man "which is done without *knowledge* is done in ignorance" (*Protagoras,* 357, p. 48). *Knowledge* then determines decisions and is the virtue of human beings (*Protagoras,* 351, p. 43):

It is a noble and commanding thing, which cannot be overcome, and will not allow a man, if he only knows the difference of good and evil, to do anything which is contrary to knowledge, but that wisdom will have strength to help him (*Protagoras,* 351, p. 43).

Toward the end of the dialogue, Plato summarized the scope of *knowledge* to be all things, "including *justice,* and *temperance,* and *courage*" (*Protagoras,* 360, p. 52), and *holiness* and thus made it the foundation of human conduct. He concluded that a virtuous person is one that adopts his *knowledge* of *justice, temperance, courage,* and *holiness* in both personal and social situations (*Protagoras,* 360, p. 52).

3.3.3 The Unity of Virtue

Plato's scope of *virtue* represents a group of ethical human qualities: *justice, temperance, holiness, courage,* and *wisdom* whose relation to one another dominates the second part of the dialogue. Socrates and Protagoras argued about if each part resembles the rest in the unity and is *knowledge* (of a kind). It is also here Plato and Protagoras reached consensus over the standards of an ideal citizen which are profound righteous qualities.

The second part of the dialogue centers on Socrates and Protagoras' debate over if *justice, temperance, holiness, courage,* and *wisdom* differ as separate types of *virtues* or are equal to one another. Protagoras first confirmed that the first three are manly *virtues* (*Protagoras,* 325, p. 17) and "are related to one another as the parts of a face are related to the whole face" (329, p. 21). Later, Socrates added *courage* and *wisdom* to the list and claimed that each type of *virtue* is *knowledge* and is related to the rest in the unity: (1) when an individual has one, he has them all (Vlastos, 1972); (2) the names of the *virtues* all refer to the same things, namely *virtue* (Penner, 1973); (3) each *virtue* is a kind of *knowledge/wisdom* (Rickless, 2003). Socrates proved his point through his infamous formula of one part is similar to the others: each part is *knowledge* (of a kind)/*virtue*.

3.3.4 Justice

The term of *justice* deserves a special attention not only because it is the first element in the unity of *virtue*s. More importantly, Plato and Protagoras both agreed that *justice* is a human inner trait that impacts an individual's decision-making and social order as a whole and thus, attached to the notion of *justice* legal significance, as laws would have.

Justice first appears as a type of *virtue* originating from the Greek mythology. *Justice* is given by Zeus who was concerned with the potential danger of race extermination (*Protagoras*, 322-323, p. 15). Zeus dispatched Hermes to distribute *justice* to all men to share in "ordering principles of cities and the bonds of friendship and conciliation" (*Protagoras*, 322, p. 15). This indicates two dimensions of *justice* in Greek society: *justice* was human natural trait given by god that could be cultivated as a *virtue* and had a legal function because "cities cannot exist, if a few only share in the virtues" (which include *justice*) (*Protagoras*, 322, p. 15).

Plato did not refute Protagoras' mythical origin of *justice*, nor did he reject the role of *justice* in the Greek life. This is because Plato himself gave a very important place to the idea of *justice*. He believed the loss of *justice* resulted in "Athenian democracy ... on the verge of ruin" and maintained that the sophists' teaching contributed to the degeneration, decay, and ruin of the Athens and divided Athens into hostile camps of rich and poor, oppressor and oppressed (Bhandari, "Plato's Concept of Justice").

3.4 *Ethos* as Human Character in Aristotle's *On Rhetoric*

Aristotle (384 B.C.E -322 B.C.E) also held that rhetoric intends to influence people's decisions or judgment (II-2. 1377b; II. 18. 1). In the important work of *On Rhetoric*, Aristotle offered the basics of the systems of rhetoric that influences all subsequent rhetorical theory and practice. Consisting of three books, the work offers a general overview, providing the purposes of rhetoric, a definition, and the contexts and types of rhetoric (Book I). Aristotle discussed three means of persuasion in Book II where I located most of the key terms for examination. He introduced style and arrangement in Book III. Aristotle shared with Plato that effective persuasion requires the orator to be knowledgeable about his subjects and to possess a unity of virtuous qualities that he dubbed as *ethos*. However, Aristotle demonstrated a more pragmatic and rational perspective of human virtuous traits. He considered *ethos* one of the three rhetorical appeals in persuasion and stressed that *ethos* influences our decisions more effectively and quickly in cases "where there is no exact knowledge but room for doubt" (II. 4. 1356a). In the following discussion, I explore three important terms: *ethos*, *virtue*, and *justice* which are respectively one of Aristotle's rhetorical appeals, the key element of *ethos*, and the most important component in Aristotle's unity of *virtue*. These terms are closely related to rhetoric's influence on individuals with respect to their roles as persons and citizens.

3.4.1 Ethos: the Right Character of the Speaker

Aristotle frequently stressed that rhetoric influences human decisions (2.1.2). Aiming at social *justice*, rhetoric represents the faculty of finding the available means of persuasion (I. 2. 1355b) through forensic oratory, democracy by means of deliberation, and extortion of the honorable in public ceremony. Among the three means of persuasion, that is, pathos, logos, and *ethos*, Aristotle explained that *ethos* refers to such qualities of the speaker/individual: attitudes, sensibilities, and beliefs and argued that in addition to pathos and logos, people also look up to the speaker' enduring traits for their judgment because such qualities affect how a person sees, acts, and indeed lives (Sherman, 1989, Introduction). He asserted that if the speaker had the three elements of *ethos*, that is, practical wisdom, *virtue*, and good will, he would make much difference in persuasion (II.1.1378a).

How does *ethos* influence persuasion? In Chapter One of Book II, Aristotle explained:

> ...the speaker seems to be a certain kind of person and that his hearers suppose him to be disposed toward them in a certain way and in addition if they, too, happen to be disposed in a certain way [favorably or unfavorably to

him]; ...for the audience to be disposed in a certain way [is more useful] in lawsuits; for things do not seem the same to those who are friendly and those who are hostile, nor [the same] to the angry and the calm but with altogether different or different in importance... It appears that it will come to pass and will be good; but to an unemotional person and one in a disagreeable state of mind, the opposite (2.1.4).

Aristotle portrayed explicitly that the speaker with a good character (calm, friendly, emotional...) presents appeal to his audience in different rhetorical contexts.

Aristotle then provided three elements of *ethos*: *practical wisdom*, *virtue*, and *good will* (II.1.1378a), among which he valued *virtue* the most. He briefly mentioned that *practical wisdom* means prudence that can be understood as man's reasoning ability in deliberation (II.1.1378a). The speaker/individual would "make mistakes in what they say or advise through [failure to exhibit] ... [or] ... form opinions rightly" (II.1.1377b). Like scientific *knowledge*, *practical wisdom* is the rational part of soul. He did not give a definition of *good will* as the concept is self-explanatory.

3.4.2 (The Unity of Mental) Virtue(s)

Virtue is the one element of *ethos* that Aristotle stressed more than the other two parts put together. He identified *virtue* in two categories: *virtue* of the body which includes health, beauty, strength, physical stature, and athletic prowess (I. 5.1360b) and *virtue* of the soul which refers to *justice, courage, temperance, magnanimity, magnificence*, and other similar dispositions (I. 6.1362b). Aristotle focused his discussion of *virtue* on the mental type. He emphasized that *virtue* of the mental type is the most important part of the ethical proof and a particular type of communication. He added that it not only benefits individuals in their decision-making, but also helps maintain a just, lawful, and democratic society (Kennedy, 1994, Prooemion).

Aristotle also connected the concept of *virtue* with human happiness, arguing that human happiness is a combination of *virtue* and success. He explained that in a just, lawful, and democratic society, "individuals privately and all people generally" pursue "self-sufficiency in life ... accompanied with the ability to defend and use" "the abundance of possessions" (I. 5.1360b), which suggests the role of *justice* in securing individuals and all people of their legal rights to cherish happy life and protect their properties.

In addition, Aristotle believed that a speaker should play his role in the audiences' pursuit of success. He pointed out that the speaker's responsibility particularly that of a political and epideictic orator is to understand the objectives and values of human life in order to be able to demonstrate a course of action in the best interest of the audience. The speaker especially "show[ed] a great sense of urgency toward knowing and doing what is morally right and gives higher priority to the contemplative life than to active political life" (Kennedy, 1991, p. 62). This virtuous character of the speaker is not just geared into persuasion as a part of the ethical proof. More importantly, it intends to a higher mission–to bring the sense of what is morally right or wrong. Therefore, *virtue* is the ability for doing good for others and a habit (I. 9.1366b) that humans cultivate through experience. It guides a good life and "comprise[s] just and decent ways of living as a social being" (Sherman, 1989, Introduction, p. 1).

Aristotle connected *virtue* with legal compliance and considered a virtuous quality for individuals to abide by the law in their pursuit of their happiness:

> ...a virtue by which all, individually, have what is due to them and as the law requires, "people perform fine actions in times of danger and as the law orders and obedient to the law", people behave as the law orders in regard to the pleasures of the body, and lack of control [is] the opposite. [It is also] a virtue productive of great benefits [for others], ...productive of something great [without little-mindedness and stinginess]. [It is also] of intelligence whereby people are able to plan well for happiness in regard to the good and bad things that have been mentioned earlier (I. 9.1366b).

Here, Aristotle emphasized that *virtue* is also helping the others and the ability to make intelligent and right decisions.

3.4.3 Justice in Association with Written and Unwritten Law

Aristotle prioritized *justice* over any other elements in the unity of *virtue* (I. 6.1362b). He defined *justice* as fairness and argued that *justice* (together with its opposite, "injustice" or "just" versus "unjust") is closely related to both written and unwritten (moral) laws for maintaining social order and offered ways for the cultivation of *justice* (I. 9.1366b, 13.1373b).

Aristotle claimed that just and unjust actions are related to both specific written and unwritten laws (I. 13.1373b). The specific and written law "...has been defined by each people in reference to themselves" (I. 13.1373b), such as violent assault and theft while the unwritten law is the values and beliefs involving "an abundance of virtue and vice, ...reproaches and praises and dishonors and honors and rewards" (I. 13.1374a). In relating *justice* to formal laws and individual virtuous cultivation, Aristotle stressed the combined significance of *justice* of the human soul and *justice* of the law in impacting both individuals and society.

In Chapter 13, Book I, Aristotle further equaled fairness to *justice* and suggested ways to cultivate this moral quality. He listed what he considered to be fairness: forgiving of human weaknesses, looking up to the legislator (or the characters of the judicial and/or the deliberative rhetor according to my interpretation), and the intent of the legislator (1374b). In other words, the awareness of *justice* can be presented in helping the others and obeying the law.

3.5 Cicero's *Ideal Orator* in *De Oratore*

Roman rhetoricians embraced and enhanced the notion of the Greek *virtue/ethos* and Marcus Tullius Cicero (106 B.C.E. - 43 B.C. E.) was one of the most representative spokesmen in this respect. He not only recognized the significance of rhetorical practice, oratory in his term, in public life of the state, but also went beyond what Plato and Aristotle stressed as the speaker's virtuous qualities or the ethical proof in rhetoric to argue that orators should have a wide *knowledge* in all the important subjects and arts they spoke about (*De Oratore*, II. 5) and civil rights in particular. He raised the bar to the height that only the *ideal orator* would meet the qualifications. Consequently, the following discussion focuses on my findings of his notion of an *ideal orator* in his book of *De Oratore* and key terms of *knowledge* and *knowledge of public law* that surround the term of *ideal orator,* to demonstrate Cicero's perception of the role and quality of the speaker in persuasion–his power and ability to shape individuals and bring social changes after–a brief introduction of his work *De Oratore*.

Cicero discussed the concept of an *ideal orator* in his treatise on rhetoric, *De Oratore*. This book is generally regarded as "Cicero's most complete, mature statement of his views on rhetoric" (Bizzell and Herzberg, 2001, p. 286) where he promoted his understanding of the quality of an *ideal orator* through his teacher and main spokesman, Crassus. Presented in the form of a dialogue like Plato's *Protagoras, De Oratore* mainly portrays the virtuous qualities of an *ideal orator* and takes him as the moral guide for the state which was undergoing "chaotic conditions and the attendant anxieties about the future" (Wood, 1988, p. 42) when the Roman Republic (506 B. C. E.~27 B. C. E.) was going through its last years.

3.5.1 The Ideal Orator: Knowledge about All Subjects

Cicero emphasized that the orator must be "broadly learned so as to elevate the audience to make it prefer the most moral solutions to common problems" and "the orator has the obligation to direct "more audience to right action" (Bizzell and Herzberg, 2001, p. 35-36).

According to Cicero, oratory derives its beauty and fullness from *knowledge*. He claimed that only those who have the *knowledge* about his subject being addressed would be able to speak with "far more weight and eloquence", which resonated with Plato in *Gorgias* (I. XI. 47). He added that even for an orator to speak only at a trial, or in the public assemblies, or the Senate-house, "he cannot engage, with the requisite cleverness and skill, even in these restricted activities" "without *knowledge* of human nature and character" (I. XI. 48). This demand of acquiring the wide *knowledge* lies in the importance of oratory to individuals, society, and the state:

> There is to my mind no more excellent thing than the power, by means of oratory, to get a hold on assemblies of men, win their good will, direct their inclinations wherever the speaker wishes, or divert them from whatever he wishes. In every free nation, and most of all in communities which have attained the enjoyment of peace and tranquility, this one art has always flourished above the rest and ever reigned supreme (*De Oratore*, I. Viii).

What is particularly worth noticing is that Cicero lauded the power oratory can give to a person, the power for an individual to maintain his rights and security, protect himself from peril as well as the state when "a complete" orator could "uphold not only his own dignity, but the safety of countless individuals and of the entire State" (I. Viii.) which Cicero considered the moral responsibility and quality of an ideal orator.

Cicero extended the *ideal orator*'s responsibilities and virtuous quality beyond the regular oratorical contexts of the courts, the assemblies, and the senate, challenging the restriction (I. X. 44) of these contexts that exclude such arts as ancient ordinances, the customs, religious rites, ceremonies, and rules of private law (I. X. 39). He insisted that the *ideal orator* must have the *knowledge* of moral science, the human life, and conduct, the *knowledge* he believed to be the orator's forever province, and philosophy's third branch. Cicero maintained that without the knowledge of these aspects, the orator would never be a great one.

3.5.2 Knowledge of Public Law

In addition, Cicero stressed the social responsibility of an *ideal orator* "must also be acquainted with *public law*, which is exclusively concerned with the State and Empire, and also the records of past events and the precedents of antiquity" (I. XLVI.). He believed that *knowledge of public law* was useful in all of the three types of rhetorical contexts:

> ... in cases and proceedings relating to private interests, his language must often be borrowed from common law. ... A knowledge of common law is   indispensable to the orator; just so, in public causes, alike in the law-courts, in

popular assemblies and in the Senate, all this story of old times, the precedents of public law, and the method and science of State administration should be material, as it were, at the disposal of those orators who occupy themselves in politics (I. XLVI).

The *knowledge of public law* is connected with an orator's moral duties to "expose to the indignation of fellow-citizens, and restrain by punishment, the crimes and iniquities of the guilty; who also by the shield of his talent, can deliver innocence from legal penalties" (I. XLVI).

My findings also indicated that Cicero did not limit the role of an *ideal orator* to the individual level; he argued that the orator could make a much bigger impact at the social level:

[He] again can either inspire a lukewarm and erring nation to a sense of the fitting, or lead them away from their blundering, or kindle their wrath against the wicked, or soothe them when they are excited against good men; who lastly can by his eloquence either arouse or calm, within the souls of men, whatever passion the circumstances and occasion may demand (I. XLVI).

Obviously, Cicero was asserting that an *ideal orator* who had the *knowledge* of his subjects and *public law* would be able to speak effectively in any given speaking contexts, whether it is in the courthouse or the assemblies or the Senate-room. More importantly, he would control crimes and bring innocence to individual citizens and leads people to the direction of *justice*.

3.6 Chinese Rhetorical Tradition: Confucianism and Daoism

China enjoys a rich rhetorical tradition dating back to a few thousand years in history (Peng, 2004; Lu, 1998; Kennedy, 1998). However, it was in the sixth century B. C. E. when the prosperous and stable West Zhou Dynasty (1046 B. C. E.~771 B. C. E.) went in decline and was replaced by Spring (722 B. C. E.~481B. C. E.) and later Warring States (475B. C. E.~221 B. C. E.) where various schools of ancient Chinese thought flourished unprecedentedly. It was the age of political, social, and military unrest, just as the name of the dynasty suggests. However, it was also the age that various schools of thought emerged, contended, and incorporated one another's perceptions into their own. Consequently, early Chinese rhetorical practice presented a mixture of a rich yet complex tradition characterized by its own political, social, and cultural circumstances. Among these schools are the famous Confucians and Daoists who, over the history, have co-existed, attacked, and influenced each another, but have permeated the Chinese life. Like their Greek counterparts, the Confucian and Daoist rhetoricians recognized the impact rhetoric makes on both individuals and society in general. However, ancient Chinese rhetoricians prioritized individuals' virtuous characters over anything else in persuasion and thus advocated adamantly moral cultivation and individual self-perfection to bring social changes, even though each school defined *virtue* in its own way.

Confucianism and Daoism interpreted *virtue* very differently. Confucianism insisted on establishing *ren*, meaning *benevolence*, and believed that *benevolence* and *benevolent governance* would restore and maintain social stability if individuals could observe the Zhou *li*, rituals and propriety of the previous dynasty, and cultivate individual moral perfection (Lu, 1998, 2000; Berrell and Wrathall, 2007). Daoist *virtue* rejected human intrusion and insisted that following the *Dao*, the Way of Nature, would lead to social order. For example, Daoists identified *de* (virtue), *wu wei* (*in-action*) and *bu zheng* (*non-contention*) to be virtuous characters in interpersonal communication, responding to the environment, solving social chaos (Cai, 2006). Apparently, Confucianism and Daoism maintained differing perceptions of human *virtue*; however, they both placed responsibilities on the shoulders of the individual for social change and believe that the individual's cultivated morality would eventually bring society back to harmony.

To present a comparable study, the following discussion focuses on the Confucian concept of *virtue* represented by *ren* and surrounding terms of *li, zheng ming,* and *cardinal relationships* from Confucius, *ren* and *ren governance* by Mencius, and the concept of *Dao,* supported by *de, wu wei* and *bu zheng* developed by Lao Zi. Then, I also compare and contrast Western and Chinese *virtue/ethos* and discuss its potential impact on how the two cultures view legal practice that includes copyright.

3.6.1 Ren and Li: the Core of Confucius's Virtue in *The Analects*

Confucianism represents the mainstream of classical Chinese rhetoric with Confucius (551 B. C. E.~479 B. C. E.) as the founder. His work, the *Analects*, which recorded Confucius' acts and words and was compiled by his students and disciples, is generally considered a book of moral philosophy, although his sayings are about many topics. Confucius believed speech and conduct of *ren* (*benevolence*, sincerity, goodness, gentility, and love) was the most important human character corresponding to a Being (Yao, 2004), believing that as long as all people submitted to *ren,* humans would live in harmony and peace. Finding ideal examples of *ren* in the old sage kings of the Zhou Dynasty, he advised rulers and social elites to follow the Zhou *li,* rituals and norms he believed to have brought prosperity and peace. He further proposed *zheng ming* and *cardinal relationships* as major strategies in practicing *li*. Consequently, cluster analysis of the Confucian *virtue* is the focus of the following discussion and *li*, together with *zheng ming* and *cardinal relationships* are the surrounding terms to be analyzed.

3.6.1.1 Ren: the Human Virtuous Character

My research findings indicated that *ren* represents the highest moral characters in the Confucius system of *virtue*. Having defined *ren* directly and indirectly for over a hundred times, Confucius stressed that the loss of *ren* caused social problems of wars and moral decay in his time and thus urged individuals, especially rulers and social elites to achieve moral perfection of benevolence. His call for *ren* responded to the political and social chaos in the Spring and Autumn Period when he witnessed disastrous "wars among small kingdoms over land and political power", "moral corruption of government officials, and a lack of direction concerning social and human development (Lu, 1998, p. 156). Consequently, he cherished a ritualistic and an orderly Zhou Dynasty and admired how the sage kings' governance kept social stability.

Confucius identified *ren* as the ultimate noble ends for an ideal society: "If the will be set on *virtue*, there will be no practice of wickedness" (*The Analects,* 4. 4.; trans. by Legge, 1891). When a benevolent person speaks/writes, he emphasizes the truthfulness of his speech and combines his speaking with *ren*. Confucius aimed especially at rulers and social elites who he believed have a greater impact on people, the community, and the state. He pointed out that if the ruler governs virtuously, the state will be in good shape:

> If a prince is able to govern his kingdom with the complaisance proper to the rules of propriety, what difficulty will he have? If he cannot govern it with that complaisance, what has he to do with the rules of propriety? (Trans. by Legge, 1891, 4.13)

He truly believed that a benevolent man was superior and only thought of *virtue*, sanctions of law, was "true to the principles of our nature and the benevolent exercise of them to others". (*The Analects*, 4.15.2)

I also found that Confucius divided people into two types based on the concept of *ren*: the superior (*jun zi*) and the base (*xiao ren*) men. The superior men always know *virtue*, despise money, love learning and people, respect authority, and strive for virtuousness (*The Analects*, 13. 25; 7. 2, 3, 20, 22; 1. 14; 6. 20; 16. 9; 4.4; 12. 16; 1.2, 6, 8, 11; 7.3, 13, 26, 12, 16). They always perfected themselves by pursuing "gravity, generosity of soul, sincerity, earnestness, and kindness" (*The Analects*, 17.6; Trans. by Legge, 1891) for:

> If you are grave, you will not be treated with disrespect. If you are generous, you will win all. If you are sincere, people will repose trust in you. If you are earnest, you will accomplish much. If you are kind, this will enable you to employ the services of others.(*The Analects*, 17.6; Trans. by Legge, 1891)

On the contrary, the base people are about personal benefits. He is conversant with gain (*The Analects,* 4. 16) and acts with a constant view to his own advantage (*The Analects,* 4. 12): personal comfort and favor that Confucius despised and condemned.

If *ren* represents the ultimate moral end, the means to achieve it is through observing the (Zhou) *li* which leads to other important terms in *The Analects*.

3.6.1.2 Li: Zhou Rituals and Codes of Conduct

Li, in *The Analects*, refers to the rituals, propriety, and code of conduct of the Zhou Dynasty that Confucius admired and advocated but was in decline in his time (Li, 1994; Xu, Chen & Liu, 1992). Closely associated with *ren*, *li* is mentioned seventy five times in the book. Viewing *li* as means to achieve *ren* and relying on rulers and social elites to extend the two concepts to the entire society,

Confucius offered *zheng ming* (rectifying names) and *cardinal relationships* for his project.

My findings indicated that Confucius knew thoroughly well about the *li* of Zhou—from land law to corporal punishment to music and to drinking vessels used in worshipping and various ceremonies. He regarded *li* as the perfect and inviolable norm to govern human behavior (Yum, 2007, p. 16) and therefore, should be obeyed as law:

> To subdue one's self and return to propriety is perfect virtue. If a man can for one day subdue himself and return to propriety, all under heaven will ascribe perfect virtue to him. Is the practice of perfect virtue from a man himself, or is it from others? (*The Analects*, 12.1.1)

In his speeches, Confucius assured his audiences that *zheng ming* would cure the problem of social and cultural degradation and rectify all other existing and potential immoral conducts. He thus rationalized his claim: power and duties were attached to the names. Once individuals knew their position and followed the Zhou *li*, society would restore past prosperity and harmony. He thus described the causal relationships in the following quote:

> If names be not correct, language is not in accordance with the truth of things. If language be not in accordance with the truth of things, affairs cannot be carried on to success. (*The Analects*, 13.3.5) When affairs cannot be carried on to success, proprieties and music will not flourish. When proprieties and music do not flourish, punishments will not be properly awarded. When punishments are not properly

awarded, the people do not know how to move hand or foot. (*The Analects*, 13.3.6)

He held strongly that not rectifying names would bring about all kinds of disastrous consequences the state had been suffering.

The other significant rhetorical strategy Confucius offered is the cardinal interpersonal relationships that arrange persons in hierarchy according to their political and social status: ruler/minister, father/son (*The Analects*, 12, 11; Trans. by Legge, 1891) and were later extended to husband/wife, older brother/younger brother as well as to friend/friend. Except friendship, all other relationships are hierarchical. Confucius believed that when these relationships are straightened, every individual knows his obligations and responsibilities within family and beyond. He would extend this awareness to public affairs he is involved in. Consequently, when everybody takes his family and social responsibilities, society would be in good shape.

This relationship system assumes dual responsibilities for the individual: filial love and piety for his parents and elders and loyalty to the state. To Confucius, "filial piety and fraternal submission" is the "root of all benevolent actions" (*The Analects*, 1. 2. 2): if all men pay filial love to their parents and elders, "there are few who, being filial and fraternal, are fond of offending against their superiors. There have been none, who, not liking to offend against their superiors, have been fond of stirring up confusion" (*The Analects*, 1. 2. 1). He maintained that the *cardinal relationships* exert a more positive influence on individuals and entire society through individual moral self-cultivation and education than legal restrictions and punishment (*The Analects*, 2. 3). Confucius' effort eventually convinced Emperor Wu (140 B. C. E.~88 B. C. E.) of West Han Dynasty to institutionalize Confucianism and make it the state orthodox doctrine.

In conclusion, a document analysis of *The Analects* indicated that Confucius regarded *ren* as the ultimate end of human ideal. To realize this goal, he proposed the Zhou *li,* claiming that following the *li* would restore and maintain societal disorder. Confucius then developed *zheng ming* and *cardinal relationships* to cultivate filial and social responsibilities in individuals, identify their obligations and duties, as well as regulate and harmonize interpersonal relations and social order.

3.6.2 Mencius: Benevolent Governance as the Mencius Primary Virtue of the Ruler

Mencius (390 B. C. E.~305 B. C. E.) purported and enhanced Confucius' legacy of cultivating *virtues* and moral characters through building *ren* and observing *li.* Therefore, *ren* and *li* are also the key terms in his work of *Mencius* that deals with "such subjects as metaphysics, psychology, human nature, ethics, politics, and language" (Lu, 1998, p. 171). These subjects intertwine with rhetoric in the formats of prose essays and arguments based on appeals to the authority of sage rulers of antiquity. However, in contrast to Confucius' general and vague teachings, Mencius offered humane rulership and pragmatic strategies to develop qualities of *ren* in individuals. These qualities are abating punishment, reducing taxes, improving crop yields, and ensuring that people are trained in moral cultivation. Consequently, he transformed Confucius' abstract concept to realistic actualization. He strongly supported moral cultivation of people, especially of the ruler and the social elites whose virtuous character had a greater and positive impact on the moral well being of ordinary citizens and social stability in general than formal legal practice. The following presents findings of *Mencius'* ren and *li* system that outlines his view of benevolent governance, strategies for practicing *li* and the cultivation of human *ren* nature.

3.6.2.1 Ren as Benevolent Governance

Mencius resonated with Confucius in his interpretation of the concept of *ren,* giving a similar definition of love, benevolence, "filial piety, fraternal respectfulness, sincerity, and truthfulness" (*Mencius*, I. 1. 4. 3) and mentioned the concept for approximately one hundred and fifty times in his work of 35,000 characters. However, he placed more responsibilities and hope on the shoulder of the rulers, stressing that benevolent governance was the virtue and determining factor for achieving social order.

In multiple chapters of *Mencius,* Mencius stressed the vital importance for the ruler to develop *ren* when he was asked for advice regarding governance by the kings:

> The King Xuan of Qi said, "What virtue must there be in order to attain to royal sway?" Mencius answered, "The love and protection of the people; with this there is no power which can prevent a ruler from attaining to it".
> (*Mencius*, I. 1. 4. 3)

Mencius again connected a ruler's prosperity with his people's joy and sorrow:

> When a ruler rejoices in the joy of his people, they also rejoice in his joy; when he grieves at the sorrow of his people, they also grieve at his sorrow. A sympathy of joy will pervade the kingdom; a sympathy of sorrow will do the same: in such a state of things, it cannot be but that the ruler attain to the royal dignity. (*Mencius*, I. 1. 4. 4)

Mencius also stressed a reciprocal relationship between the ruler and his people, claiming that if the ruler cared about his people, his people would return that care to him. He believed that if the sovereign was benevolent, all would be benevolent: if the sovereign was righteous, all will be righteous (*Mencius*, IV. 2. 5). This has been proved by the experience of former sage rulers: King Yao, King Shun, and King Wen who run their governments with benevolence (*Mencius*, IV. 1 & 2).

3.6.2.2 Li as Issuing Beneficial Policies for the Public

However, Mencius did not just repeat Confucius' *ren* by means of following the Zhou *li*. He urged the rulers to share with his people happiness, hardships, and worries to show sincere *ren* to them. The following is some of his realistic and persuasive strategies of *ren* governance:

> Let mulberry trees be planted about the homesteads with their five mu (Chinese system of area measurement, approximately equals to 1/3 acre), and persons of fifty years may be clothed with silk. In keeping fowls, pigs, dogs, and swine, let not their times of breeding be neglected, and persons of seventy years may eat flesh. Let there not be

taken away the time that is proper for the cultivation of the farm with its hundred mu, and the family of several mouths that is supported by it shall not suffer from hunger. Let careful attention be paid to education in schools, inculcating in it especially the filial and fraternal duties and grey-haired men will not be seen upon the roads, carrying burdens on their backs or on their heads. (*Mencius*, I. 1. 1. 3)

Here, Mencius was persuading the ruler that loving and protecting the people was characteristic of a benevolent government, the *virtue* of a ruler, and the sure path to royal dignity – he persuaded his audience that safety and prosperity of a state rely on a benevolent government.

3.6.2.3 Ren as Human Nature and its Cultivation

My research revealed Mencius' rhetorical perspective is also embedded in his philosophical views. However, he differed from Confucius who seemed to solely focus on the building of *ren* through observing *li* without arguing for the feasibility of his project. Mencius adamantly claimed that humans by nature possessed benevolence, righteousness, propriety, and knowledge as their limbs, and therefore, may easily exercise *ren* (*Mencius*, VII. 1. XV. 1-3).

Mencius was positive about humans' ability to improve themselves and create a better world because "[a]ll men have a mind which cannot bear to see the suffering of others" (*Mencius,* II. 1. 4. 1). He also took ancient sage kings as moral models for the rulers: "The ancient kings had this commiserating mind...They... had likewise a commiserating government. When with a commiserating mind and government, to rule the kingdom was as easy a matter as to make anything go round in the palm"(*Mencius*, II. 1.6. 2). He encouraged the rulers and social elites to become Yaos and Shuns who were sage kings: "... repeat the words of Yao, and do the actions of Yao, and you will just be a Yao" (*Mencius*, VI. 2. 2. 5), because sage kings had all the necessary and moral rituals and standards (*Mencius*, VII. 1).

How does an individual talk reflect the speaker's moral character? Mencius propagated moral speeches that he categorized into good speech (simple, easy to understand, but has profound significance), benevolent speech (speech that conforms to *ren* and *li*), as well as sincere speech (that is based on reality and truth): "Words which are simple, while their meaning is far-reaching, are good words". (*Mencius*, VI. II. XXXII.1) Mencius did not give an explicit definition of benevolent speech, but he did stress following the examples of ancient sages in whatever you do may include speaking benevolent speeches. However, he emphasized clearly the significance of substantial speech: "words which are not true are inauspicious, and the words which are most truly obnoxious to the name of inauspicious, are those which throw into the shade men of talents and virtue." (*Mencius*, IV. II. XVII.1)

Mencius promoted the conformity between benevolent speaking and conduct, and offered pragmatic ways of observing the *li*. He relied more on the ruler for social change, believing *benevolent governance* would set the moral example for the people, and brought social harmony.

3.6.3 Daoism: the Way, the Virtue, In-Action, and Non-Contention of Lao Zi's *Dao De Jing*

Daoism represents a rival school of thought to Confucianism that has also permeated Chinese culture. My findings indicated that

Daoism expressed in *Dao De Jing* by Lao Zi rejects the Confucian effort to alternate individual behavior through moral propagation and purposeful actions. Instead, it asserted that following the rule of nature, the *dao* by cultivating *de* (*virtue*) through the ways of *wu wei* (*in-action*) and *bu zheng* (*non-contention*) would restore social harmony (*Dao De Jing*, Chapters 1, 2, 3, 4, etc., Trans. by Legge, 1891). Consequently, the presentation of the findings focuses on the key term of *Dao/Tao* (the *Way* of Universe/Nature), and then *de* (*virtue*), *wu wei* (*in-action*), and *bu zheng* (*non-contention*) that cluster around *Dao* to examine how the Daoist rhetorical practice.

3.6.3.1 Dao: The Law of Nature

Dao De Jing is the canonical work of *Daoism* written by Lao Zi, a senior contemporary of Confucius whose real name is Er Li but the date of his birth and death is little known. Composed of only 5,000 words, the book is divided into *Dao Jing* (Canon of *Way*) and *De Jing* (Canon of *Virtue*), suggesting its topics of "the *Way*" and "*virtue*" while discussing a prudential mundane life philosophy, political and military strategies, as well as advocating a naturalist attitude toward the cosmos (Lu, 1998, p. 227). Lao Zi stressed the significance of the *dao*, mentioning it for more than seventy times throughout the book. He believed that *dao* creates and brings all things into existence in nature and thus *dao* represents the central concept of Daoism which humans must align themselves with in order to achieve a happy life.

My findings illustrated that *dao* by Lao Zi refers to an timeless force that has produced Heaven, Earth, and other things (*Dao De Jing*, I. 1 & L.1) and is characterized by its eternity and ultimate power:

The Tao produced One;

One produced Two;
Two produced Three;
Three produced all things.

Dao begets and governs all things. *Dao* is also nameless, aimless, invisible, and beyond the ability of ordinary language to describe: The Tao [*dao*] that can be spoken of is not the eternal Tao; the name that can be named is not the eternal name (*Dao De Jing*, I. 1, Trans. by Legge, 1891).

Because of the complicatedness, *dao* can only be spoken of indirectly through various metaphorical, paradoxical, and mysterious expressions. Examples are all things under Heaven come into being from concrete things and all beings come into being from the invisible *Dao* (*Dao De Jing*, XL. 4). "The Valley Spirit never dies ... [Her] doorway ... is the base from which Heaven and Earth sprang" (*Dao De Jing,* VI, Trans. by Wang and Jiang, 2006).

3.6.3.2 De (Virtue): The Actualization of the Dao

De, meaning *virtue*, represents "the fulfillment of *dao* through wise speech and proper action" (Lu, 1998, p. 230). Having been mentioned for forty four times, *de* is the second most frequently stressed term after *dao*. These two terms are intricately related to each other as ends and means similarly like *Ren* and *Li* and cannot be treated separately: "The *Tao* [*dao*] begets all beings, and *de* fosters them. The *Tao* and *de* give them form, and the environment makes them accomplished. Therefore, all beings, without exception, venerate the *Tao* and value *De*" (*Dao De Jing,* LI. 1; Trans. by Wang and Jiang, 2006).

Lao Zi discussed two types of *de*: mysterious quality (*Dao De Jing*, X. 4) and constant *virtue* (*Dao De Jing*, XXVIII. 1-2). Mysterious quality refers to the ability to produce and preside over all without claiming the presence (*Dao De Jing*, X. 3; Trans. by Legge, 1891): "It produces all, yet makes no claim; it does all, yet does not boast; it presides over all, yet does not control." (*Dao De Jing*, X. 3) The constant *virtue* refers to simplicity, purity, and non-interference found in the quality of a baby before he loses his innocence, a raw material before it is carved to become a vessel, and the sagely practice that does not take violent measures (*Dao De Jing*, XXVIII. 1-3). Lao Zi used these analogies to encourage his audience to rid themselves of desires and remain wise and empty like the sages who managed affairs by "non-action" and taught "without saying thing" (*Dao De Jing*, II. 3). This leads us to the next major concepts of *wu wei (in-action* and spontaneity) and *bu zheng (non-contention)* that are the concrete manifestations of *de* to actually conform to the *Dao*.

3.6.3.3　Wu Wei and Bu Zheng: the Manifestation of *De*

Wu wei and *bu zheng* (*in-action* and *non-contention*) are two closely related rhetorical strategies Lao Zi proposed as the most effective solution to the then political, social, and moral chaos. He argued that refraining from the attempt to control things that are beyond a person's control and thus harmonizing with the environment without contention would bring about the desired effect. This perspective rejected the Confucian doctrines of *ren* and *li* which relied on rectifying names and using hierarchy to organize interpersonal relationships and society.

Wu wei means doing nothing opposed to nature. That is, *the dao*, rather than doing nothing. Lao Zi regarded the rule of nature governs all things in its own order that could not and should not be defied. Any human imposing of his wills only "generates rigid patterns of response [while] sacrificing spontaneity at the social and individual levels" (Lu, 1998, p. 231). He claimed:

> A state may be ruled by punishment;
> Weapons of war may be used with skill;
> But the whole world may be gained by freedom from action
> and purpose.
> The multiplication of prohibitions increases the poverty of
> the people.
>
> The more implements to add to their profit that the people
> have, the greater disorder there is in the state
> (*Dao De Jing*, LXVII. 1 – 2).
> ... ...

The more legislation there is, the more thieves and robbers there are. He emphasized: "The *dao* invariably does nothing, and yet there is nothing left undone. If dukes and kings could preserve it [the *dao*], all things would submit to them spontaneously." (*Dao De Jing,* XXXVII; Trans. by Wang and Jiang, 2006)

Lao Zi proposed *bu zheng* (*non-contention*) as the other evidence of *de* to approach the *dao*. As mentioned in the previous discussion, Lao Zi maintained that the *dao* is the ultimate control of all things and human interference only causes the abandonment of the *dao*. He laid the blame on Confucius, accusing him that *ren* and *li* result in the abandonment of the *dao*; knowledge and wisdom cause hypocrisy; filial piety and parental affection cause families to lose harmony;

loyal ministers caused country disorder (*Dao De Jing,* XVIII. 1; Trans. by Wang and Jiang, 2006). *Bu zheng* is a better solution because "a good man does not prove things by argument; he who proves things by argument is not good" (*Dao De Jing,* LXXXI. 2; Trans. by Wang and Jiang, 2006).

Here, Lao Zi is saying that a virtuous person should not spend his time and energy on verbal contentions. Instead, he should remain modest and follow the example of the sages who focused on their conduct and spent and gave more to others (*Dao De Jing,* LXXXI. 4). He provided an example through the conduct of water. Water excels many other items "in benefiting all things, and in its occupying, without striving (to the contrary), the low places which all men dislike" (*Dao De Jing,* VIII. 1). Water just follows the rule of nature. Hence (its way) is near (that of) the Tao (*dao*). Analogously, people should behave like water and do good things for others without claiming the credit.

3.7 Western and Chinese Concept of *Virtue/Ethos* and its Potential Impact on U.S. and Chinese Legal (Copyright) Approaches: A Comparison and Contrast

The above findings emphasized the notion of *virtue/ethos* and other related terms in the ancient Greco-Roman and Chinese rhetorical practice primarily represented in six texts. Now, I move to the comparison examining their similarities and differences, as well as the concept's possible influence on U.S. and Chinese legal (copyright) approaches.

3.7.1 Similarities: Virtue/Ethos' Significance

Both of the Western and Chinese rhetorical traditions revealed in the key terms examined identified the significance of *virtue/ethos* ancient Western and Chinese rhetoricians recognized in shaping individuals and society. This similarity indicates their common expectations for virtuous individuals and an ideal society, which, in Burke's term, would be an identification of acceptable values and beliefs.

Plato and Aristotle held that *virtue* is a unity that encloses different aspects. Plato considered each of *virtue* a type of *knowledge* and human quality that assists individuals in distinguishing good from evil. Aristotle viewed *virtue* a part of the personal character, the ethical appeal of a persuasive speaker. He enriched Plato's scope of *virtue* and added the elements of magnanimity and magnificence to Plato's list which allowed the individuals to consider altruism in their communication with other people. Cicero established a higher standard for the orator. He maintained that an *ideal orator* should not only have the knowledge of all the subjects that he addressed, but also that of moral science and public law, holding that virtuous character could defend his own dignity and uphold the safety of countless others (I. VIII).

The Chinese rhetoricians weighed *virtue* as much as their Western counterparts. The Confucian approached *virtue,* or *ren* as the ultimate end of human pursuit for a happy and harmonious life. To this end, the Confucians proposed *li,* the Zhou rituals and norms that, they considered effective means. Confucius offered the strategies of rectifying the names and the cardinal relationships to regulate individuals' personal and social obligations. Mencius relied on the ruler for social change, believing that as long as the ruler governed with benevolence and issued policies beneficial for his people, social harmony would be restored and maintained. Daoism, on the contrary, took the opposite path. Completely rejecting Confucian *ren* and *li*, Lao Zi, regarded the Confucian system of *virtue* a human intrusion into the natural law of the universe, the *dao*. Instead, he proposed inaction and non-contention as rhetorical strategies to re-establish political, social, and moral order of individual persons and the state.

3.7.2 Differences: Justice versus Human Control and the Way of Nature

Although both Western and Chinese ancient rhetorical traditions cherished *virtue/ethos* in persuasion and human decision making, Western *virtue/ethos* as indicated in the major terms Plato, Aristotle, and Cicero used stresses legal awareness of individuals and connects with formal law that are intended to regulate individual conduct and social order. Using Burke's notion of terministic screen, I contend that such an approach to *virtue/ethos* implies that individual virtuous qualities cannot single-handedly eliminate social problems or bring order to society. Only when virtue combines with formal laws will it have the best influence on individuals and society. In the Chinese case, Confucius, Mencius, and Lao Zi extolled the impact of *virtue/ethos*, screened out the significance of formal laws in regulating human behavior and maintaining social order, and totally relied on individual moral consciousness for social stability and order.

Western rhetorical practice represented by Plato, Aristotle, and Cicero all connected the concept of *virtue/ethos* with formal legal practice. Plato agreed with Protagoras that *justice* as a human *virtue* is innate in human character given by god. The awareness of justice is used to order cities and regulate human relations and communication (*Protagoras*, 322. p. 15). Aristotle had *justice* as the first element of his unity of *virtue* (I. 6.8.) and pointed out it was related to written and unwritten laws (I. 13. 1.19) that ordered principles for social *justice* and used moral values to distinguish from good and bad (I. 13. 1. 19). Cicero viewed public law as required knowledge and social duty exclusively concerned with the State and Empire for an ideal orator (I. XLVI.). With his legal *knowledge,* the orator was able to deliver innocence and restrain by punishment. (*De Oratore*, I. XLVI).

Chinese rhetorical tradition as presented in document analysis recognized individual virtue awareness the effective way to realize social order. The Confucians represented by Confucius and Mencius held that *ren* was the ultimate end of individual moral cultivation. They maintained that if individuals themselves were aware of their own obligations, they would automatically obey social rules. Confucius believed that rectifying names and cardinal relationships clarified individual obligations, regulated individual behavior, and thus would ultimately solve social issues. Mencius extended filial love to governance: if a ruler ruled his country with benevolence by adopting beneficial policies, his people would treat him with respect (I. I. 5, Trans. by Legge, 1895). Daoism completely rejected Confucius' proposition of individual moral cultivation, claiming that Confucius' approach of *ren* and *li* human intrusion that interferes with the rule of nature that Lao Zi recognized as the *dao* (63.1). He proposed the means of inaction and non-contention (73. 2) that he believed to be the best solution to social problems.

Such a disparity in the Western and Chinese approaches to *virtue/ethos* may affect their perspective of legal (copyright) practice. The U.S. culture has inherited Western rhetorical tradition and may tend to rely on formal law enforcement to protect copyrights while stressing the impact of individual virtue awareness. Chinese culture that continues the legacy of Confucian and Daoist rhetoric would prioritize individual moral cultivation over formal legal measures in the regulation of individual behavior toward copyright protection because both schools maintained that law and punishment may or may not eliminate crimes and failed to bring involuntary compliance with rituals and norms. Consequently, the effectiveness of protection in China might not meet U.S. standard.

3.8 Conclusion

This chapter has discussed the notion of *virtue/ethos* in Western and Chinese rhetorical practices. Focusing on six texts, the discussion featured a cluster analysis of the concept and those that are related to *virtue* in the two cultures. The chapter also briefly compared and contrasted their similarities and differences regarding the meaning the significance of *virtue/ethos* in the two cultures and the influence on copyright practice. The findings indicated Western rhetorical practice represented by Plato, Aristotle, and Cicero all enclosed legal aspect in *virtue*. Plato and Aristotle asserted *justice* was the most important virtuous human character and adding formal legal practice in their discussion of *justice* while Cicero pointed out that *an ideal orator* must have the *knowledge* of public law so that he could assist his audience in their decision-making in all oratory contexts.

On the contrary, ancient Chinese rhetorical tradition represented by the Confucians focuses on building *ren* by means of following the example of ancient sages. Confucius and Mencius believed as long as an individual understood his obligations within the family, he would not likely to defy his authorities. The rulers, in particular, should serve as a moral model for the public. However, Lao Zi rejected Confucius' *virtue* of *ren*. Maintaining that individual moral cultivation is a human intrusion, Lao Zi proposed following the natural flow of the *dao* without action or contention. Such an approach rejected formal legal practice and viewed individual moral cultivation as the only effective way to regulate people and country. Consequently, copyright that provides formal legal protection of individual intellectual rights, conflicts with Western perspectives of law and individual private properties. As a result, Chinese tend to be tolerant of copyright piracy.

In the next chapter, my discussion will focus on cultural dimensions and their potential impact on the U.S.-China legal or copyright approach. Next chapter will explore cultural values and beliefs and their potential impact on U.S.-China copyright approaches.

Chapter Four
The Impact of Cultural Traditions on the U.S. and China Legal/Copyright Approaches—the Cultural Dimensions

4.1 Introduction

This chapter, the second data analysis chapter, addresses three cultural dimensions, that is, universalism/particularism, individualism/collectivism (communitarinism), and low/high power distance. Applying the method of intercultural rhetoric/communication, the chapter also studies how these cultural orientations impact the way U.S. and Chinese cultures view legal/copyright practice. As discussed in previous chapters, both cultures inherit a rich rhetorical tradition. These rhetorical traditions reflect themselves in "[separate cultural] values, ideas, and other symbolic-meaningful systems as factors in the shaping of human behavior and the artifacts produced through behavior" (Hofstede 2000, p. 9, quoted in Kroeber and Parsons, 1958, p. 583).

Data analysis in this chapter also seeks to understand the association between rhetorical traditions, the above-mentioned three cultural dimensions, and legal/copyright approach by mears of using the approach of intercultural rhetoric/communication. I first focus on key values, ideas, and beliefs that are manifest in later Western/U. S. and Chinese texts through presenting their meanings and then their connections with cultural dimensions. These texts are:

- The *Declaration of Independence* (the *Declaration*)
- The *Constitution of the United States of America* (*The U.S. Constitution*)
- The *Constitution of the People's Republic of China* (*China's Constitution*)
- *Deng Xiaoping's Southern Tour Speeches* (*Deng's Speeches*)

Then, I explore the potential influence of these cultural dimensions on the two cultures' approaches to legal (copyright) practice. In other words, data analysis in this chapter attempts to answer the question of "*what cultural values, ideas, and beliefs have a sustaining impact on how the U.S. and Chinese view legal (copyright) practice?*"

4.2. U.S. Cultural Dimensions: Cultural Values and Beliefs Revealed in the *Declaration of Independence* and the *U.S. Constitution*

The *Declaration of Independence* and the *U.S. Constitution* are two of the most important documents in the U.S. history. Proclaimed in 1776, the *Declaration* birthed a new and unique nation which can be seen in the immensity of its impact on world history and the growth of democracy in the U.S. ("Declaration of Independence: A History"). In addition, the *U.S. Constitution* sets the foundation for the U.S. legal system and the government and valorizes the spirit of the *Declaration*. My data analysis indicated that these two documents present core U.S. beliefs and values illustrated in the dimension of universalism, individualism, and low power distance identified by researchers such as Hampden-Turner, Trompenaars (2000) and Hofstede (2001). A close examination found the following outstanding U.S. beliefs and values:

- Life
- Liberty (personal, political, and economic freedom)
- The pursuit of happiness
- Independence
- Common good
- Justice

- Equality
- Diversity
- Popular sovereignty
- Rule of law
- Separation of powers/checks and balances

The values and beliefs are revealed throughout the texts of the *Declaration* and the *Constitution*, indicating their significance in the view of the founding fathers of the country.

Before we examine how these values are associated with U.S. cultural variability and now they impact the culture is approach to copyright, we must understand their meanings. The following interpretation of U.S. cultural values is my adaptation based on Collison et.al.'s explanation (2003) released on the Michigan State's government website that sheds light on the three cultural orientations.

Individuals have the inviolable right to life except in certain highly restricted and extreme circumstances, when the use of deadly force is to protect one's own life or the lives of others.

Liberty refers to an unalterable aspect of the human condition. Included in this idea are three types of freedoms: personal, political, and economic. Personal freedom allows a private realm for individuals to act, think, and believe freely. Economic freedom gives individuals the right to acquire, use, transfer, and dispose of their private properties without unreasonable governmental interference. It is also the right to seek employment wherever one pleases, to change employment at will, and to engage in any lawful economic activities. Political freedom represents the right to participate freely in the political process, to choose and remove public officials, and to be governed under a rule of law. It also includes the right to a free flow of information and ideas, open debates, and the right of assembly.

Independence refers to choice provided to people, choice to do things of one's own will without control. For the pursuit of happiness, while individuals have their own way to pursue happiness as long as they do not infringe upon others' rights. Common good represents interests for both individuals and people of the U.S. as a whole:

> ...to form a more perfect Union, establish Justice, insure domestic Tranquility, provide for the common defense, promote the general Welfare, and secure the Blessings of Liberty to ourselves and our Posterity, do ordain and establish this Constitution for the United States of America.
> (*The U.S. Constitution*)

Justice is the notion that individuals should be treated fairly in the distribution of the benefits and burdens of society, the correction of wrongs and injuries, and in the gathering of information and making of decisions. Therefore, all citizens should be treated equally in the aspects of political, legal, social, and economic life.

The United States is a pluralist country with a variety of cultures, races, ethnic backgrounds, beliefs, and life styles which are permissible and beneficial. The citizenry is collectively the sovereign of the state. It holds ultimate authority over public officials and their policies.

Virtuous citizens display devotion to their country through loyalty to the fundamental values and principles upon which the U.S. depends. They should exhibit a reasoned commitment to the core democratic values through their words and deeds.

The government and the governed should both be subject to the law. Legislative, executive, and judicial powers are exercised by different institutions independently in order to maintain limitations placed upon them. The powers given to the different branches of government must be balanced and roughly equal so that no branch can completely dominate the others. Branches of government are also given the ability to check the power of other branches.

These values and beliefs are inherited from the Western rhetorical tradition that emphasizes *justice*, rule of law, and social order, and are enhanced in the typical U.S. context. They exemplify features of cultural dimensions Hampden-Turner and Trompenaars (2000) as well as Hofstede (2001) have identified in their empirical research. I use these features as a basis of departure for my research approach.

4.3 Universalism, Individualism, and Low Power Distance: U.S. Cultural Dimensions and Values and Beliefs

Hampden-Turner and Trompenaars (2000) and Hofstede (2001) identified U.S. culture as universalistic, individualistic, and low power distance orientated based as its major characteristic features. According to Hampden-Turner and Trompenaars (2000), U.S. culture tends to impose universal rules on all people and stresses compliance with written law and rules, a practice that unites U.S. citizens of diverse backgrounds. The culture has an "I" focus that values competition, self-reliance, individual growth, and fulfillment. It also underscores equal rights and opportunity and highly regards individual achievements rather than social status. *The U.S. Constitution* and *the Declaration* that I chose to examine reveal ample examples of values and beliefs that support these researchers' assumptions (See Table 4.1 below). As a result, the following discussion will focus on the findings of these values and beliefs and their association with U.S. cultural dimensions.

Table 4. 1   The U.S. Cultural Dimensions, Features, and Supporting Values and Beliefs

U. S. Cultural Orientations	Cultural Features	Values and Beliefs
Universalism	Universal rules, written law, and a new system for all	Life, liberty, the pursuit of happiness, rule of law, equality, patriotism, balance and check of power, justice
Individualism	"I" focus on competition, self-reliance, individual growth and fulfillment	Life, liberty, the pursuit of happiness, rule of law, equality, popular sovereignty, justice, diversity
Low Power Distance	Equal rights and opportunity, emphasis on individual achievement rather than social background	Equality, pursuit of happiness, life, liberty, justice, common good

The Declaration of Independence and *The U.S. Constitution* revealed outstanding values and beliefs that support U.S. cultural orientation of universalism that Hampden-Turner and Trompenaars identified in their research (2000). The most significant ones in *The Declaration of Independence* are life, liberty, and the pursuit of happiness. The American colonists claimed these values to be universal and therefore, they "hold these truths to be self-evident, that all men are created equal, that they are endowed by their Creator with certain unalienable Rights, that among these are Life, Liberty and the pursuit of Happiness" (*The Declaration of Independence*, Introduction). The American colonists held these rights to be divine and endowed to humans from their birth. These rights protect the life of individuals and allow them to cherish political, economic, and personal freedoms. These rights are universal and any violations should be addressed immediately. These rights were consistency in *The U.S. Constitution* whose aims are "provide for the common defence, promote the general welfare, and secure the Blessings of Liberty..." (Preamble, Amendments 1-10).

The rights to life, liberty, and the pursuit of happiness are related to the notion of the rule of law which is indicative of U.S. universalism in both of the two documents researched. The word law is the second most frequently mentioned term (54 times) after the United States (72 times) in *The U.S. Constitution*. In the *Declaration of Independence*, the word law is mentioned 10 times (See Table 4. 2 below). The rule of law assumes that everyone is governed by rules and regulations regardless of who they are, meaning equal legal treatment for all. For instance, the *Declaration of Independence* makes it clear that the British king abused the Americans' "unalienable rights" and thus petitioned for a response:

He has refused his Assent to Laws, the most wholesome and necessary for the public good.

> He has forbidden his Governors to pass Laws of immediate and pressing importance, unless suspended in their operation till his Assent should be obtained; and when so suspended, he has utterly neglected to attend to them.

He has refused to pass other Laws for the accommodation of large districts of people, unless those people would relinquish the right of Representation in the Legislature, a right inestimable to them and formidable to tyrants only.

... ...

(*The Declaration of Independence*).

The king's violations have brought "injuries and usurpations" and caused "patient sufferance" to the Americans. Therefore, he was deemed a tyrant and an unjust ruler.

Table 4. 2   Universalist Terms Frequently/Intensely Mentioned in the U.S. Texts

Terms	Frequency/intensity in the *U.S. Constitution*/the *Declaration*
Law	54/10
Right(s)	22/13
Just/justice	7/6
Equal/equality	8/2

To promote the rule of law, the *U.S. Constitution* provides the legal framework that not only gives power to the legislature, the presidency, and the judiciary; it also checks and balances the power to prevent corruption. In doing so, the *U.S. Constitution* attempts to build and maintain a more equal and just society that colonial Americans claimed the British rule failed, so that people of a diverse ethnic background would be loyal to the fundamental values and principles of the newly established country.

The "I" focus also exemplifies the concept of individualism (Hampden-Turner and Trompenaars, 2000; Hofstede, 2001). In the

Declaration of Independence, individual natural rights to life, liberty, and pursuit of happiness are stressed. The movement toward independence assumed that its success would assist individual Americans in their achievement of these rights, rights suggesting self-reliance, individual growth, and fulfillment. Consequently, the *U.S. Constitution* advocates these rights through its emphasis on personal, political, and economic freedoms, allowing individuals to think and act freely, shape their destiny, and make their own decisions (*The U.S. Constitution,* Third Amendment):

> Congress shall make no law respecting an establishment of religion, or prohibiting the free exercise thereof; or abridging the freedom of speech, or of the press; or the right of the people peaceably to assemble, and to petition the Government for a redress of grievances. (*The U.S. Constitution,* First Amendment)

In addition, the *U.S. Constitution* further specifies the protection of individual privacy and economic interest/property:

> The right of the people to be secure in their persons, houses, papers, and effects, against unreasonable searches and seizures, shall not be violated, and no Warrants shall issue, but upon probable cause, supported by Oath or affirmation, and particularly describing the place to be searched, and the persons or things to be seized. (*The U.S. Constitution,* Fourth Amendment).

The respect for individual intellectual property is also evidenced by the Congress' effort "[t]o promote the Progress of Science and useful Arts, by securing for limited Times to Authors and Inventors the exclusive Right to their respective Writings and Discoveries" (*The U.S. Constitution*, Article I, Section 8, Clause 8). Historical and cultural connections between the U.S. and Great Britain suggest that the U.S. has inherited Britain's tradition of copyright practice regardless of its refusal to protect foreign copyrights for more than 100 years after it issued its first copyright act in 1790. The short clause of copyright protection, on the one hand, considers public access to literary, artistic, and scientific information and knowledge. On the other hand, it secures individuals' intellectual property rights and motivates them for future creations and innovations so that individuals could realize their individual growth and fulfillment through fair competition.

Self-reliance, individual growth, and fulfillment need a level playing field where the law secures equal rights and opportunity access in competition. My data analysis found that the *U.S. Constitution* has a specific section, the Bill of Rights, devoted to individual rights. This section emphasizes personal, political, and economic privileges for U.S. citizens which include freedom of religion, press, speech, petitioning the government for responses to grievances (*The U.S. Constitution*, Amendment 1), and protection of property (*The U.S. Constitution*, Amendment 5). The Bill of Rights also incorporates equal legal treatment. For instance, the amendments rule that in criminal and civil cases, the accused should enjoy the right to both speedy and public trials by an impartial jury, and no excessive fine, bail, or cruel punishment should be inflicted (*The U.S. Constitution*, Amendment 6 & 7).

The emphasis on fundamental rights also indicates human equality and tolerance of diversity that a popular sovereignty promises and the rejection of social hierarchy. Various values and beliefs illustrate the U.S. low power distance cultural orientation. The Americans are a people from diverse ethnic backgrounds who have severed with the Old World and challenged the authority for human justice:

> We hold these truths to be self-evident, that all men are created equal, that they are endowed by their Creator with certain unalienable Rights, that among these are Life, Liberty and the pursuit of Happiness. To secure these rights, ... whenever any Form of Government becomes destructive of these ends, it is the Right of the People to alter or to abolish it, and to institute new Government, laying its foundation on such principles and organizing its powers in such form, as to them shall seem most likely to effect their Safety and Happiness.

These values and beliefs defy the practice of hierarchy and inequality which Hofstede and Hampden-Turner and Trompenaars view as a feature of low power distance (2001) or achievement culture (2000). Having gained independence and freedom from "absolute Despotism" and "absolute Tyranny" (*The Declaration of Independence*), an autonomous state must check and balance the power of the government branches to avoid the charges it once placed against the British rule. To that end, the *U.S. Constitution* specifies that "[t]he President, Vice President and all civil Officers of the United States, shall be removed from Office on Impeachment for, and Conviction of, Treason, Bribery, or other high Crimes and Misdemeanors" (*The U.S. Constitution*, Article II, Section 4).

Another interesting example illustrates the U.S. rejection of hierarchy. *The U.S. Constitution* prohibits any officials holding office from accepting "any present, Emolument, Office, or Title, of any kind whatever [without the Consent of the Congress], from any King, Prince or foreign State", nor would the United States grant any title of nobility (*The U.S. Constitution*, Article 1, Section 9). This suggests the effort "to form a more perfect Union, establish Justice, insure domestic Tranquility, provide for the common defence, promote the general Welfare, and secure the Blessings of Liberty to ourselves and our Posterity" (*The U.S. Constitution*, Preamble).

U.S. cultural values and beliefs discussed above illustrate the orientations of universalism, individualism, and low power distance. These cultural dimensions cherish rule of law for all and strive to provide level playing fields for individual competition, fulfillment, and human equality, which differ from Chinese cultural practice as revealed in the Chinese documents I examined and will discuss below.

4.4 Chinese Cultural Dimensions: Cultural Values and Beliefs Revealed in the *Constitution of the People's Republic of China* and *Deng Xiaoping's Southern Tour Speeches*

China's Constitution and *Deng's Speeches* are among the most important contemporary Chinese documents. *The Constitution* offers guidelines for China's current political, economic, legal reforms, and corresponding practice, as well as defines individual rights and duties. *Deng's Speeches* rationalizes the imperative to carry on the economic reform policy and persuades the central government to continue the effort.

Like the *U.S. Constitution*, *China's Constitution* is the highest law that provides legal framework for the country and structure of the state, and clarifies fundamental rights and duties. It was first issued in 1949 when the Communist Party won the civil war over the Nationalist Party led by Chiang Kai-Shek. *China's Constitution* has been revised four times and the latest amendment became effective in 2004. *Deng's Speeches* were released in 1992 about two and a half years after the Tiananmen Democratic Movement. At the time, Westernization which was introduced by market economy and radically expressed in student demonstrations, raised skepticism about China's reform and concerns for possible consequences. The *Speeches* are highly accepted in China and have been considered to have emancipated the Chinese minds, accelerated the pace of reform and opening up, as well as strengthened economic construction in Chinese history. These two major Chinese texts revealed the following core values and beliefs that I chose to demonstrate the three cultural dimensions identified by Hampden-Turner and Trompenaars (2000) and Hofstede (2001):

- Patriotism/nationalism
- Socialism (with Chinese characteristics)
- "We" focus/collectivism
- Peace and harmony
- Public and collective ownership
- Individuals' rights

- Individuals' duties
- Loyalty to the ruling party

Before I examine the association between these values and beliefs and cultural dimensions, I first present how these values and beliefs are approached in China. Then, I explore their connection with Chinese cultural orientations followed by their implications on Chinese perspective of copyright practice.

In current Chinese context, patriotism refers to loyalty to the country and the ruling party. It ranks number one of the Chinese values and beliefs in both documents. The notion is frequently and intensely stressed through both indirect reference and explicit emphasis in the two texts. For example, terms that are connected with patriotism and regularly mentioned are "People's Republic of China", "China", "Chinese of all nationalities", and "our country/nation". Patriotism is also in citizens' loyalty to *The Constitution* and the realization of modernization in China (*China's Constitution*; *Deng's Speeches*). For example, the Constitution states:

> All political parties and public organizations and all enterprises and undertakings in the country must take the Constitution as the basic norm of conduct, and they have the duty to uphold the dignity of the Constitution and ensure its implementation (*China's Constitution,* Preamble).

This requirement is based on the claim the Chinese people of all nationalities "led by the Communist Party of China...overthrew the rule of imperialism, feudalism and bureaucrat capitalism, won the great victory of the new-democratic revolution and founded the

People's Republic of China" and became for the first time "masters of their country" (*China's Constitution*, Preamble).

Socialism with Chinese characteristics is the basic national policy (*Deng's Speeches*; *China's Constitution*). It refers to the combination of Communist Party dictatorship and Western market economic practice. It also exhibits China's unique political, economic, and social circumstances as different from other nations in the world.

Collectivism or "we" focus emphasizes equality, unity, and common prosperity for all group members. It has always been the major Chinese cultural value. For example, the "Specific Economic Zones" in South China aimed to "prosper" those regions first by means of market economic communication with Hong Kong, Taiwan, and the world. The ultimate goal was to bring common wealth to the entire country through enhancing capitalist economic experiment in the rest of the country. This practice is a common collective approach in China's reform policy since late 1970s and was particularly popular in the 1980s and 1990s.

The emphasis on peace and harmony is typical characteristic of Chinese culture inherited from ancient times when *ren* and *li* were enforced through rectification of names and hierarchical relationships, as well as obedience without action (*The Analects*; *Mencius*; *Dao De Jing*). In current China, the ruling political party carries this legacy by upholding its dictatorship, which prohibits any political contentions challenging its supremacy. The leaders believe that if China changes the political system, China will encounter a domestic war and social chaos (*Deng's Speeches*; *China's Constitution*).

The two types of economic system China practices are public and collective ownerships. Public ownership is the primary type and the collective is complementary. As a result, the state and the collective own the right to all natural resources and properties including the lot upon which private properties are built (*China's Constitution*). The public and collective ownerships shape general Chinese public's approach to resources they have access to: all belong to the state and the collective or the people, and individuals sacrifice their interests for the benefit of the public, which resonates with China's rhetorical tradition of altruism I previously mentioned about.

Individual rights refer to political and social equality that every Chinese citizen enjoys. *China's Constitution* claims that every individual citizen has the freedom of religious belief, speech, the press, assembly, association, procession, and demonstration (Chapter Two, Articles 36-37), as well as many other rights, regardless of race, gender, age, and social status. In addition, they have the right to criticize, make suggestions to, and complain about the government, as well as place charges through legal process against the government without any retaliation (*China's Constitution*, Chapter Two, Article 41).

Chinese cultural values emphasize individual duties. In the *Constitution*, individual duties go side by side with individual rights and constitute Chapter Two of *China's Constitution*. These duties include the obligations to work, rest, safeguard the unity of the country and integrity of all nationalities, abide by *China's Constitution* and other laws, and honor the interests of the motherland (*China's Constitution*, Chapter Two, Articles 53-55). In addition, the duty also includes filial respect of adult children for their aging parents in the manner of taking care of the parents:"children who have come of age have the duty to support and assist their parents" and "maltreatment of old people ... is prohibited" (Chapter Two, Article 49). This is another typical cultural legacy from the Confucius time.

These values and beliefs indicated the significant influence of Chinese rhetorical tradition discussed in previous chapter. They provide examples for the cultural variables Hampden-Turner and Trompenaars (2000) and Hofstede (2001) have identified in their empirical research and are related to Chinese approach to copyright practice I discuss later in this chapter.

4.5 Particularism, Collectivism, and High Power Distance: Chinese Cultural Dimensions and Values and Beliefs

Contrary to U.S. cultural orientations of universalism, individualism, and low power distance, Chinese culture tends to be more particularistic, collectivistic, and high power distance oriented (Hampden-Turner and Trompenaars, 2000; Hofstede, 2001). My findings indicated cultural features that echoed with what Hampden-Turner and Trompenaars and Hofstede identified as examples of China's cultural dimensions. These features are "we" focus and collectivist orientation that stress altruism and self-sacrifice, uniqueness and incomparability emphasizing context, and tolerance of hierarchy and inequality based on social status (Hampden-Turner and Trompenaars, 2000, p. 68, 24, 198-202; Hofstede, 2001, p. 227, 98; Beamer and Varner, 2001; Samovar, Porter, and McDaniel, 2006; also see Table 4. 3. below). There are ample examples of these features in the two documents.

China's Constitution and *Deng's Speeches* revealed values and beliefs that support the country's particularistic cultural orientation Hampden-Turner and Trompenaars identified in their research (2000). The major evidence lies in the political system it adopts: socialism with Chinese characters or Chinese-style socialism which significantly dominates modern Chinese life.

Table 4. 3   Chinese Cultural Dimensions, Features, and Supporting Values and Beliefs

Chinese Cultural Orientations	Cultural Features	Values and Beliefs
Particularism	Uniqueness and incomparability of people, situations, and events	Socialism with Chinese characteristics
Collectivism	"We" consciousness of altruism and public service	State and collective ownership, patriotism/nationalism, peace and harmony
High Power Distance	Hierarchy and inequality based on social status, domination of the powerful	Ruling party's dictatorship, loyalty to the ruling party, individuals' duties and obligations

In *China's Constitution* which is composed of 16,498 Chinese characters, the word socialism is mentioned forty-seven times, ranking the fourth most frequently stressed term. In *Deng's Speeches*, which consisted of 8,007 Chinese characters, it appears thirty-three times. Socialism with Chinese characters suggests a combination of socialism and capitalism. The former refers to China's political system and the latter is the country's capitalist economic practice. The combination indicates the uniqueness of the culture in which two paradoxical ideologies coexist. This practice assumes that China has its own political, economic, and social characteristics which are different from other countries in the world and consequently, it chooses systems that fit the Chinese situation, indicating a consideration of context and particularism. The system, on the one hand, legitimizes the continuing dictatorship of the Communist Party in a capitalist economic practice. On the other hand, it responds to the exigency for the economic reform which sustains the ruling party's sole control over the country when living standards are constantly improving and China undergoes modernization.

I contend that such a unique practice is a modern-day *zheng ming* that resonates with the Confucian proposition of rectifying names for social order and thus, justifies dictatorship by using economic initiatives that improve living standard and enhance modernizations. *China's Constitution* thus explains socialism with Chinese characters:

> The basic task of the nation ... is to concentrate its effort on socialist modernization. Under the leadership of the Communist Party of China and the guidance of Marxism-Leninism and Mao Zedong Thought, the Chinese people ... will continue to adhere to the people's democratic dictatorship and follow the socialist road, steadily improve socialist institutions, develop socialist market economy and democracy, improve the socialist legal system and work hard and self-reliantly to modernize industry, agriculture, national defence and science and technology step by step to turn China into a socialist country with a high level of culture and democracy (*China's Constitution*, Preamble) .

China's Constitution here emphasizes the adherence to current socialist practice characterized by Communist Party leadership and the effort to realize four modernizations. Deng Xiaoping, the then Chinese leader, also rationalized this uniqueness that blends contradictions (*Deng's Speeches*):

> Some people argue that the more foreign investment flows in ... the more elements of capitalism will be introduced and the more capitalism will expand in China ... The proportion of planning to market forces is not the essential difference between socialism and capitalism. A planned economy is not equivalent to socialism, because there is planning under capitalism too; a market economy is not capitalism, because there are markets under socialism too.

Socialism with Chinese characters illustrates the uniqueness of Chinese cultural practice. It maintains orthodox socialism in political practice while experimenting with capitalism in economic activities, indicating an exception and a feature of particularistic consideration of contexts.

The two documents also indicate strong "we" consciousness that prioritizes altruism, public service, as well as patriotism which are features of the collectivistic cultural orientation (Hampden-Turner and Trompenaars, 2000; Hefstede, 2001). Values and beliefs that emphasize the unity of and equality between all nationalities, or ethnic groups, for societal harmony through the protection of the rights and interests of all people especially support the dimension of collectivism:

> The state upholds and develops the relationship of equality,

unity and mutual assistance among all of China's nationalities. Discrimination against and oppression of any nationality are prohibited; any acts that undermine the unity of the nationalities or instigate their secession are prohibited (*China's Constitution*, General Guidelines, Article 4).

In addition, the *Constitution* also makes it clear that any "treasonable" or "counter-revolutionary activities" would be suppressed and penalized (*China's Constitution*, General Guidelines, Article 28). The armed forces will take the tasks of suppressing and punishing treasonable and counter-revolutionary activities by strengthening national defense, resisting aggression, defending the motherland, and safeguarding the people's peaceful labor (*China's Constitution*, General Guidelines, Article 29).

Table 4.4 Collectivistic Terms Frequently Mentioned in the Chinese Texts

Terms	Times Appeared in *China's Constitution/Deng's Speeches*
People	371/18
People's Republic of China	80/0
Country	151/16
Socialism	47/33
We	0/60
China	32/15

I also found terms of collectivist values are frequently and intensely stressed. For example, the word "people", suggesting collective interests, appears more than three hundred times. Other words or terms, such as "China", "country", "we", and "People's

Republic of China" also make frequent appearances in either the *Constitution* or the *Deng's Speeches* or both (See Table 4. 4. above). Some terms may not be directly proclaimed or frequent themselves as often as those I previously mentioned, but they carry such intensity that ignoring them would miss important examples of the collectivistic orientation of China. These terms include but are not limited to "patriotism", "state and collective ownership", "individuals' duties" or "obligations", and "common prosperity". All these terms intend to promote national or collective interests.

The analysis of the documents indicated that group interest and patriotism are among the top Chinese values emphasized in the Chinese texts. In fact, the entire preamble of the *Constitution* functions as patriotic education through a brief narration of China's contemporary history. The preamble consists of 1,792 Chinese characters as opposed to the short 27-word preamble of *The U.S. Constitution* (The English translation version is 1,071 words). The historical narration stresses China's "splendid culture and glorious revolutionary tradition" that includes Chinese people's "heroic struggle for national independence and liberation and for freedom" in the 19th century when China was reduced to semi-colonial and semi-feudal society after the 1840 Opium War. Next, it mentions the termination of the feudal monarchy and the birth of the Republic of China under the leadership of Dr. Sun Yat-sen in 1911 while pointing out the limitation of Dr. Sun's revolution that failed in "overthrowing imperialism and feudalism" (*China's Constitution*, Preamble). Then, the preamble stresses the ultimate success of China's revolution led by the Communist Party of China (CPC) that "overthrew the rule of imperialism, feudalism and bureaucrat capitalism", built "the new-democratic" dictatorship in 1949 and let "the Chinese people

[take] state power into their own hands and [become] masters of the country" (*China's Constitution*, Preamble).

The last part of the preamble also conveys the message of patriotism in the emphasis on China's unprecedented achievements under the CPC's leadership. These achievements concern multiple fields: the political, economic, national defense, education, science, and technology, etc. Then, the emphasis switches to China's current national goal that highlights economic construction, adherence to the sole leadership of the CPC, the reform and opening up, and political/ideological approach (socialist system, Marxism, Leninism, and Mao Zedong Thought). One single sentence states the purpose of *China's Constitution* in the preamble which calls on all Chinese, individuals and organizations, armed forces and enterprises, to "take *China's Constitution* as the basic norm of conduct" (*China's Constitution*, Preamble) because "[the Chinese] have the duty to uphold the dignity of *China's Constitution* and ensure its implementation" (*China's Constitution*, Preamble). Thus, *China's Constitution* functions partly as a moral awareness education through a collectivistic perspective that teaches all the Chinese to pay their loyalty to the country and the ruling party that represents China.

Deng's Speeches also provide examples of collectivist interest:

> To take the road to socialism is to realize common prosperity step by step. Our plan is as follows: ... some areas may develop faster than others; those that develop faster can help promote the progress of those that lag behind, until all become prosperous. If the rich keep getting richer and the poor poorer, polarization will emerge. The socialist system must and can avoid polarization. ... [T]he

areas that become prosperous first to support the poor ones by paying more taxes or turning in more profits to the state.

Such is typical Chinese collectivism which prioritizes group benefit to individual interests. The realization of such practice is often through propaganda and moral awareness education.

Other important collectivistic values peculiar of Chinese culture lie in the texts' emphasis on the practice of the state and collective ownership systems. *China's Constitution* elaborates on the two main economic systems China adopts: "the basis of the socialist economic system of the People's Republic of China is socialist public ownership of the means of production, namely, ownership by the whole people and collective ownership by the working people" (General Guidelines, Article 6-10). These systems rule that state ownership is the "leading force in the national economy" which "ensures the consolidation and growth of the state economy" (*China's Constitution*, General Guidelines, Article 8). Consequently, all natural resources, such as waters, forests, mountains, grassland, unclaimed land, beaches as well as land in the cities belong to the state with the exception of those that are the properties of the collectives (*China's Constitution*, General Guidelines, Article 9). "Land in the rural and suburban areas, ... house sites, private plots of cropland and hilly land are all owned by the collectives" (*China's Constitution*, General Guidelines, Article 10). *Deng's Speeches* indicated that even in those Special Economic Zones like Shenzhen, "the publicly owned sector is the mainstay of the economy, while the foreign-invested sector accounts for only a quarter" (*Deng's Speeches*). The dominance of state and collective ownership leaves little room for individual interests.

The stress on the CPC's exclusive leadership exemplifies

Chinese's acceptance of hierarchy and unequal distribution of power which are features of high power distance cultural orientation (Hofstede, 2001) and a Chinese cultural legacy. Hofstede's research indicated that China has a higher power distance index than both the Asian and world average (from Hofstede website). According to him (2001), high power distance cultures tolerate hierarchy and regard inequality acceptable in both family and social contexts. The emphasis on the exclusive leadership of the CPC over the country defines China's high power distance orientation in the political sphere and the influence of this practice permeates in all walks of Chinese life. *China's Constitution* states that the CPC has led China onto the road of socialism after it achieved the ultimate success of "overthrowing imperialism, feudalism, and bureaucratic-capitalism" (*China's Constitution*, Preamble) and established the People's Republic of China. When current China is experiencing socialist construction, the CPC will maintain its dominating role:

> [U]nder the leadership of the Communist Party of China and the guidance of Marxism-Leninism, Mao Zedong Thought, and the "three represents", [has] formed ... a broad patriotic united front ... composed of democratic parties and people's organizations...[T]he Chinese people of all nationalities will continue to adhere to the people's democratic dictatorship and follow the socialist road, steadily improve socialist institutions, develop socialist democracy, improve the socialist legal system... (*China's Constitution*, General Guidelines)

China's Constitution gives credits to the CPC and legitimizes the ruling party's complete entitlement to the role of leadership.

In the quote, the "three represents" stand for the CPC's self extolling assessment:

> The CPC represents the vanguard of the Chinese working class, ... has always represented the development trend of advanced productive forces, [and] the orientation of advanced culture and the fundamental interests of the overwhelming majority of the people in China. ("The 'Three Represents Theory'", 2001)

The "three represents" send an explicit message to other political parties and the general Chinese public that the CPC deserves the leadership position in China and legitimizes it. Consequently, hierarchy is created to which all other political bodies and Chinese citizens are supposed to yield. In such circumstances, it is easy to understand why judicial procedures are not independent and government of different levels or officials could interfere with decision making. *Deng's Speeches* echoed this emphasis. He insisted that "throughout the process of reform and opening, we must also adhere to the Four Cardinal Principles" which include the exclusive control of the CPC over the country.

Hierarchy is not new in China. Using hierarchical relationships to regulate individual behavior and social order has been a tradition promoted by the Confucians I previously described in Chapter three. Such a rhetorical influence does not only exist in the political arena. It also carries its influence in everyday life. For instance, *China's Constitution* stresses filial love. In Article Forty Nine, *China's Constitution* explicitly mentions the reciprocal obligations between parents and children: it is parents' duty to raise their young children and when parents are old, adult children must take care of their elder parents. Ill treatment of old people, women, and young children is prohibited.

Chinese cultural values and beliefs discussed above lean to particularism, collectivism, and high power distance. These cultural dimensions allow exceptions, accept uniqueness, prioritize group interests over individual benefits, and tolerate hierarchy between people of different social status.

4.6 Cultural Dimensions and Their Potential Impact on the U.S.-China Copyright Approaches: A Comparison and Contrast

Both the U.S. and Chinese documents revealed significant values and beliefs that support their cultural orientations. These differences may have an impact on how the two cultures negotiate and communicate in certain contexts such as copyright practice. Universalism, individualism, and low power distance orientation that emphasize universal laws, individual rights, and equality may shape a strong awareness of copyright protection that enhances rule of law, individual achievement, and social justice. Contrarily, particularism, collectivism, and high power distance are more likely to tolerate exceptions in law enforcement due to their consideration of context, prioritize group and collective interests at the sacrifice of individuals, emphasize individual obligations over their benefits or properties, and experience more power abuse and corruption in the process of copyright enforcement.

Universalism emphasizes sameness, similarity, and takes the effort to "impose on all members of a class or universe the laws of their commonality" (Hampden-Turner and Trompenaars, 2001, p. 14). Cultures that practice universalism may be predisposed to stress "rules, codes, laws, and generalizations" (Hampden-Turner and Trompenaars, 2001, p. 14). For instance, the *Declaration* claims that all men are equally entitled to the rights of "Life, Liberty and Pursuit of Happiness" by the Laws and Nature and the Creator. The government, then, has the responsibility to secure these rights for its people. If the government fails to fulfill its obligations or violates these rights, it should be replaced by a better one. The American colonies placed charges against the British rule, claiming that the king did not provide these basic rights, and petitioned to replace the governance with a new government that stands for the benefits of all American people.

The *U.S. Constitution* espouses with the values the *Declaration* cherishes and promises to establish and maintain a government by and for all the Americans that would secure equal rights for individuals. To these ends, government branches have separate powers as well as limits to eliminate possible abuse. The rule of law in U.S. universalism is also manifest in the emphasis on: (1) personal, political, and economic freedoms, (2) the right to protect oneself with arms, privacy, property, houses, and papers against searches and seizures, (3) equal legal treatment in trial, bail, and fines without cruel punishment, and (4) other rights not listed in the *U.S. Constitution*. In terms of personal properties which are most relevant to copyrights, Amendments 4 and 5 especially stressed that without due process of law, and private property should not be searched and seized or taken for public use.

U.S. individualist cultural orientation emphasizes "I"

consciousness and conformity to universalism (Hofstede, 2001, p. 227). Both of the two texts take as the core value that every individual has equal rights to life, liberty and the pursuit of happiness. *The Declaration* claims that human individuals are endowed with these natural rights and the abuse of which should be addressed. The American colonies charged the British government for its violation of these rights and rationalized their war of independence against Britain and built their government which would represent the interest of American colonists. The *U.S. Constitution* emphasizes the basic rights in the preamble to "establish Justice" and "secure the Blessings of Liberty to ourselves and our Posterity", as well as specifies them in the Bill of Rights. What is particularly worth mentioning is the amendments' stress on the protection of individuals' freedoms, privacy, and properties from possible violations by the state/federal government as well as the equal and fair legal treatment every citizen should be granted. This is typical of individualistic culture that underlines personal achievements and rights in decision-making for themselves (Beamer and Varner, 2001, p. 70).

Low power distance cultural dimension that emphasizes equality and rejects hierarchy tends to lean on the law for the protection of individual rights (Thatcher, 2001). In the *U.S. Declaration*, the Americans challenged British authority against unequal treatment, accusing the king of his failure to secure individual universal rights of life, liberty, and the pursuit of happiness. In the *U.S. Constitution*, equality and rejection of hierarchy are a continuing emphasis in the effort to balance and check power for the prevention of potential corruption and power abuse among government branches. The *Constitution* also highlights individual rights, such as freedoms of religion, speech, and the press. Individuals can also assemble, petition of grievances, and bear arms to protect themselves. In addition, the Bill of Rights also emphasizes equal legal treatment in both civil and criminal prosecutions through trial by jury. These values and rules illustrate the effort to bring equality, justice, and opportunities for all individuals.

To bring these cultural orientations to the context of copyright protection, I contend that U.S. culture characterized by universalism, intellectualism, and low power distance tends to view formal legal practice as an effective measure to order society, promote individual achievement, and support equal treatment. Such cultural orientations may enhance copyright protection because they allow and encourage individuals to cherish their ideals and values, stress the protection of individual rights and interests based on level playing competitions, and universalize rule of law for human equality. Moreover, the *U.S. Constitution* particularly claims that IPRs will be protected. The goal of the protection, in spite of enhancing the development of science and useful arts and ensuring public access, is to emphasize individual benefits (Article 1, Section 8, Clause 8), indicating the U.S. has a long tradition of copyright practice that balances the interests of individuals and the general public. On the contrary, China's particularistic, collectivistic, and high power distance cultural dimensions are more likely to allow exceptions rather than rule of law for all when infringing happens, prioritize public and group interests over individual benefits, and practice hierarchy. Such cultural orientations may cause less awareness of copyrights and ineffective enforcement.

Particularism runs into conflict with the universal rule of law. For example, socialism with Chinese characteristics that practices both socialism and capitalism may suffer from an ideological dilemma. When disputes concerning business and trade happen in the market economic system and are submitted for a legal settlement, the legal procedure may find it difficult to reach an independent decision in the context when a dictatorial political system imposes its influence. The two dichotomous systems will probably coexist in China for a long time as indicated in *China's Constitution* and *Deng's Speeches*. As long as one party continues to dominate the country, it will have a long way to go before a universal rule of law applies.

China's collectivistic orientation privileges group interest, "we" consciousness, altruism with public service, obligation toward family, social harmony, and patriotism and marginalizes individual benefits. Consequently, it neglects individual rights and benefits. *China's Constitution* constantly stresses individual loyalty to the ruling party and national integrity while Deng frequently emphasizes common prosperity (1992). The most significant example of China's collective cultural orientation is its economic system of ownership that completely prioritizes public interests and marginalizes individual private properties. Such a practice does not encourage individual fulfillment, nor does it promote awareness of individual rights, if not totally ignore individuality.

These Chinese cultural dimensions, when reflected in the context of copyright protection, will probably allow exceptions in legal enforcement rather than adopt universal rule of laws, prioritize group benefit at the sacrifice of individuals' private intellectual properties when extensive infringing happens, and tolerate privileges and favors instead of social justice and equality when copyright piracy happens. First, this is because particularist cultures allow exceptions. When piracy occurs, the enforcement actions may take context into consideration to allow loopholes for powerful individuals, government officials, and public benefits when they are in conflict with individual private interests. Also, state and collective ownerships as the mainstay of China's economic ownership system may lead the Chinese to approach copyrights as public or collective properties when they have an access, totally ignoring their conduct is piracy. In addition, power distance orientation may result in power abuse and corruption in copyright enforcement.

Consequently, IPRs (copyright included) as intangible private properties suffer ineffective protection. Although China "promotes the development of the natural and social sciences", "disseminate scientific and technical knowledge", and "commends and rewards" individuals for their achievements in research, discoveries, and inventions (*China's Constitution*, General Guidelines), individuals always make sacrifices for group or collective interests when extensive piracy occurs. Such a phenomenon supports what a Chinese saying states: "Law does not punish massive crimes", suggesting the in-action of the law when facing collective violations. Another example also indicates that public interests dwarf the benefits of individuals. Before copyright was issued, writers were only compensated with a little "transcription fee" for their creations (Yang, 2003) because individual persons were supposed to be selfless and altruistic and should share with the public their achievements. Even if copyright law exists, there is still a general lack of awareness.

U.S. and Chinese values and beliefs exemplify different cultural dimensions. They may influence the two cultures' respective approaches to legal/copyright practice. The U.S. culture emphasizes rule of law, individuality, and equality that may result in strong copyright awareness and effective enforcement. The Chinese particularistic, collectivistic, and high power distance orientations tend to allow exceptions, value collective interests, consider social status in legal/copyright enforcement, which may cause low awareness of and ineffective copyright protection.

4.7 Conclusion

U.S. values and beliefs indicated strong cultural dimensions of universalism, individualism, and low power distance which emphasize universal rule of law, the protection of individual rights, and equality. Contrarily, the Chinese texts revealed orientations of particularism, collectivism, and high power distance that allow exceptions, privilege collective interests, and tolerate hierarchy over rule of law, individual rights, and equality. As a result, U.S. cultural values and beliefs may enhance copyright protection while Chinese cultural dimensions are likely to tolerate piracy and, therefore, enforcement will not be as effective as what U.S. expected. In the next Chapter, I will focus on the U.S.-China copyright debate in the context of copyright/intellectual property right internationalization and globalization that may influence the two cultures' approaches to copyright practice.

Chapter Five

The U.S. and Chinese Approaches to Copyright Practice—An Ideological Criticism

5.1 Introduction

This chapter, the last of three data analysis chapters, examines the U.S.-China copyright/IP conflicts over China's copyright protection issue in early 1990s in the context of copyright internationalization and globalization. The conflicts exemplify an ideological encounter involving domination, coercion, concession, and submission which are the basic features of Marxist criticism.

Classical Marxism and neo-Gramsci hegemony in particular, have identified these features in their approaches to rhetorical texts. In addition, the encounter may reflect and have contributed to the two cultures' approaches to global copyright practice.

As mentioned in the methods chapter, the copyright approach of a country represents a collective behavior that carries the impact of many factors, such as the political, economic, and legal which have been researched by many professionals in their respective fields and briefly summarized in the first chapter. I argued that rhetorical traditions, values and beliefs, as well as the promotion of global copyright protection influence a culture's approach and therefore, proposed adding a rhetorical perspective to the study of copyright approaches of the U.S.-China. In Chapter Three, I examined Western and Chinese rhetorical traditions and their respective impact on how the two cultures approach legal (and copyright) practice. I analyzed clustering key concepts in the chosen artifacts and compared and contrasted Western and Chinese understandings of the concept of *virtue/ethos* and its implications. In Chapter Four, I focused on cultural values and beliefs, using the method of cross-cultural rhetoric/communication. Similarly, I compared and contrasted U.S. and Chinese cultural dimensions and their impact on the two cultures' approaches to copyright.

In this chapter, I focus on U.S.-China copyright conflicts in the historical context of the internationalization and globalization of IPR protection, copyright included. I use an ideological approach, specifically the method of classical Marxism and the neo-Gramsci theory of hegemony in rhetorical criticism. In data analysis below, I first introduce the development of copyright/IPR practice in the world that experienced the stages of internationalization and globalization. I also refer to representative international IPR treatises: the *Berne Convention*, the *TRIPS Agreement*, and the U. S.-China copyright conflicts in the early 1990s. This introduction is important because Marxist criticism requires the critic to locate and understand the artifacts in the historical contexts of their production and "analyze the historical conditions which produced them" (Storey, 1998; 2001; Foss, 2004). Then, I present the findings of the conflict settlement using two monumental bilateral agreements and discuss the implications of these agreements to the two cultures' copyright approaches. This treatment of the texts aims to answer the question of "How does the globalization of copyright protection influence the U.S. and China's approaches to copyright as reflected in their conflicts?" The texts are:

- *Memorandum of Understanding between the Government of the United States of America and the Government of the People's Republic of China on the Protection of Intellectual Property* (the *1992 MOU*)
- *China-United States: Agreements regarding Intellectual Property Rights* (the *1995 IP Agreement*)

5.2 Global Copyright Protection: From Internationalization to Globalization

Global copyright protection has roughly experienced two major stages represented by the enactment of the *Berne Convention for the*

Protection of Literary and Artistic Works (the *Berne Convention*) and the *Agreement on Trade-Related Aspects of Intellectual Property Rights* (the *TRIPS Agreement*) that have a binding force for all signatories and World Trade Organization (WTO) members. The *Berne Convention*, for the first time in the history of copyright practice, provides a cohesive amalgamation of international copyright law for the purpose of convenience and ease of interpretation between countries and "promise[s] the development of international standards for copyright protection" ("A Brief History of Copyright"). The *TRIPS Agreement*, enhances the *Berne Convention* by broadening the scope of copyright protection through introducing IPRs into the international trading system and making it the compulsory threshold for all current and future WTO members.

In the establishment of the two agreements, developed countries controlled the process and standard setting due to the privileges of being the founding nations of the treatises, their technological advancement, as well as expertise in IP legislation. Consequently, world IPR practice prioritizes the benefits of developed countries to those of developing ones. More specifically, major European countries dominated the development of the *Berne Convention* which represents the internationalization of copyright practice. The U.S. played a deciding role in the establishment of the *TRIPS Agreement*, and brought IP protection into world trade. Developing countries, such as China, were reduced to subordination whose interests were marginalized due to these countries' insignificant role in the process of treatise establishment, inexperience in the field of copyright legislation, and high dependency on developed countries for export trade. Therefore, such an ideological encounter of copyright globalization in China suffices a Marxist approach to understanding the features of domination, coercion, negotiation, and concession that "harmonize" the practice in the world.

5.2.1 The Internationalization of Copyright Practice: The *Berne Convention*

The *Berne Convention*, for the first time in world history of copyright protection, responded to the inadequacy of national corresponding laws in an attempt to impose an all-governing international law on nations to regulate and protect copyrights of works across national borders. It was initiated by leading European countries such as Great Britain, France, Germany, Italy, Spain, and Belgium in 1886 (Yang, 2003; Alford, 1995) and joined first by developed and then developing countries. The *Convention* bore the mark of an empire building with developed countries taking the dominant role in its establishment while developing countries were voiceless and marginalized. When the *Convention* was first promoted, the developers were the world's advanced economies that shared similar political, economic, and cultural situations (Drahos, 1995). Naturally, the protection standards mostly represented the interests of the founding states. Many other developed countries acceded to the *Convention* between the late 19th century and the 1920s. Following suit were former colonies that became members of the *Convention* in the 1960s, while most other developing countries complied with the practice over the last thirty years (List of the *Berne Convention* Members, WIPO, 2011).

The *Convention* has experienced six revisions, four of which were made before 1948, the period during which most developed countries joined in (List of the *Berne Convention* Members, WIPO,

2011). The content regarding copyright protection highlights these major principles:

- National treatment to works of authors of the member countries (Article 5. 1)
- Automatic protection without any formality (Article 5. 2) and independence of protection
- Minimum standards of protection of works and duration of protection (Article 7.2)
- Developing countries in conformity to the established practice (WIPO, "Summary of the Berne Convention...").

The *Convention* emphasizes the effort of universalizing legal practice in the field of copyright that aims to bind all signatories that participate in transactions involving copyright protection.

By the time developing countries became members after the 1960s, the *Convention* was already a sophisticated model. Consequently, developing countries found it difficult to bring in their interests due to the insignificant role they played in the development of the *Convention*. Furthermore, many developing countries were not able to contribute to the *Convention* for lack of experience. Many still did not have copyright laws. Those countries that had just established their own copyright statutes borrowed extensively from the expertise of developed countries (such as China that became a member in 1992). Accordingly, developed countries maintained their complete control over the standard setting while developing countries were just to follow the rules (Drahos, 1995).

5.2.2 The Globalization of Copyright Protection: The *TRIPS Agreement*

In 1994, international copyright practice embarked on the stage of globalization. The Uruguay Round was concluded and signed the *Agreement on Trade-Related Aspects of Intellectual Property Rights* (the *TRIPS Agreement*) (Mathur, 2003, p. 65). The *TRIPS* broadens the scope of copyright/IP protection by connecting it with the world trading system to accommodate the increasing technological involvement in world trade. The accomplishment of the *TRIPS Agreement* was made under the heavy influence of the U.S. successful lobbyism. The *TRIPS Agreement* thus became the second most important treatise binding current and future WTO members.

The *TRIPS Agreement* was a result of strong lobbyism which continuously allows the expansion of the scope of copyright/IP protection. Starting from the 1980s, the world witnessed a tremendous technological advancement and increasing trade exchanges. The U.S. became the most important information exporter in the world that finally joined the *Berne Convention* in 1989 and many of its multinationals were expanding their operations in overseas markets including China (U.S. Census Bureau, "Trade in Goods with China", 1985~1993). As a result, "rapid increase in trade and drastic shift to high-technology products led businesses, particularly multinational corporations, to voice concerns about piracy and lax intellectual property protection" (Tully, 2003, p. 132) to the U.S. government. These big businesses, especially those that have high information portfolios and operations in developing countries, persuaded the U.S. government that strong IPR protection overseas would promote U.S. values and ideas, create and preserve more jobs, and help restore a positive trade balance for the country (Drahos, 1995, p. 7-8; "The U.S.-China IP Agreement: Implications...", 1995)

The U.S. government was convinced to initiate a proactive effort on the protection of IPRs globally. It developed strong negotiation strategies through massive consensus building first with big companies to establish a high intellectual property standard at the *General Agreement on Trades and Tariffs* (GATT of the WTO) (Drahos, 1995). Then, they reached to countries that supported IP protection, such as Europe and Japan that helped shape the text of the *TRIPS Agreement*. The last group the U.S. approached was developing countries that had to accept the U.S. terms without much resistance. This is because these countries were highly dependent on the Western market and were concerned about possible trade sanctions the U.S. Special 301 Report might impose or were enforcing on them due to intellectual property infringements (Sell, 1995; Yu, 2001). Therefore, developed countries, this time the U.S. in particular, controlled the globalization of copyright protection which promotes the U.S. ideas, objectives, values, and beliefs through coercions and negotiations. Developing countries, once again, had to surrender to the domination, seemingly accepting the protection standards which were beyond their ability due to their high dependency on the market for their export goods and fear of possible trade punishment by the U.S. (Yu, 2001; Drahos, 1995; Sell, 1995).

The *TRIPS Agreement* enhanced the *Berne Convention* and promoted copyright practice/IPR protection to the global level. First, the *TRIPS Agreement* maintained the provisions of the *Berne*

Convention. More significantly, it added more provisions and thus raised protection standards with new elements regarding copyright protection (See the *TRIPS Agreement* on WTO Website):

- Computer programs and databases are added to the treaty as copyrighted materials
- Enforcement provisions of domestic procedures and remedies

The purpose of these efforts is to "reduce distortions and impediments to international trade ... promote effective and adequate protection of intellectual rights, and ensure that measures and procedures to enforce intellectual property rights do not themselves become barriers to legitimate trade" (The *TRIPS Agreement*, 1995, Preamble).

Apparently, the internationalization and globalization of copyright practice is a movement spreading from developed countries to developing nations involving domination, submission, coercion, negotiation, and reconciliation. It represents an ideological practice with developed countries controlling the process and standard setting given the privileged position these countries enjoyed from the beginning when international copyright protection was established in the world. Developing countries, on the contrary, were in a disadvantageous situation due to their absence from and insignificant role in the establishment of the *Berne Convention* and later the *TRIPS Agreement* and had to submit to the domination with tremendous reconciliations because of their dependency on the Western market and concerns about trade sanctions (Yu, 2001; Sell, 1995).

The U.S.-China copyright conflicts took place in the early 1990s in such historical moments when developed countries, represented by the U.S. in this case, were aggressively promoting internationalization and globalization of IPR protection in the world as I previously described. Developing countries did not have much voice in the process and had to accept the protection standards. Although the conditions were minimum standards, they were still beyond the ability of developing nations and could probably be met only on paper. In the U.S.-China case, conflict settlement between the two countries produced two monumental agreements, one focusing on changing China's copyright (IPR) laws and the country's accession to international conventions and the other emphasizing enforcement actions and plans to complement IPR laws. To better illustrate the ideological factor, I will briefly introduce the background of the conflicts before presenting the findings of the *1992 MOU* and the *1995 IP Agreement*. Then, I discuss the ideological encounter between the U.S. and China that reflects the two cultures' approach to copyright and potential implications.

5.3 The U.S.-China Copyright Conflicts: The *1992 MOU* and the *1995 U.S.-China IP Agreement*

This part of the discussion focuses on the U.S.-China conflicts over China's copyright protection issue in the early 1990s. It exemplified the U.S. effort to promote copyright internationalization and IPR globalization in China and the Chinese submission to the pressure, as well as marked the commencement of the two countries' debate over IP protection ever since then. The settlement produced two bilateral treatises: the *1992 MOU* and the *1995 U. S.-China IP Agreement* which highlighted China's promise to accede to the world copyright conventions, bring its relevant laws in compliance with international practice, improve legal enforcement, and open more Chinese market for U.S. businesses of copyright products, indicating the increasing pressure China faced over the issue. Both of the treatises were reached after lengthy and difficult negotiations, coercions, dominations, and compromises (Li, 2006; Yu, 2001; USTR Special 301 Reports, 1989~2011) which illustrates an ideological encounter that reflects the two cultures' approaches to copyright.

The *1992 MOU* focused on IPR legislation adjustment in China and the *1995 IP Agreement* complemented and furthered the effort of the *1992 MOU* to stress enforcement tasks and action plans. When combined, the two agreements accomplish the goal of copyright/IPRs protection legislatively, administratively, and in the aspect of enforcement. Both treatises primarily emphasized China's obligations while briefly mentioning the U.S. responsibilities, indicating that the U.S. took a dominant control in the debate while China yielded to the control most probably due to the pressure of Special 301 investigations and concerns about trade sanctions. In settling the conflicts, an unequal relationship was formed between the two parties, a relationship that classical Marxism and Neo-Gramsci would focus on in approaching texts and events. More specifically, the relationship revealed a disparity in the two cultures' protection of copyright/IPRs. Predictably, the one-sided agreements may not bring about expected protection of copyright/IPRs.

5.3.1 Memorandum of Understanding between the Government of the United States of America and the Government of the People's Republic of China on the Protection of Intellectual Property (the *1992 MOU*)

The *1992 MOU*, signed on January 17, represents the result of months of bilateral negotiations over the U.S. complaint about China's inadequate IPR legislation and ineffective protection. The U.S. accused China of infringing its IPRs, claiming that piracy caused millions of dollars of losses to U.S. businesses (*USTR Special 301 Reports*, 1989~2011). The agreement mostly highlighted China's promise to amend its current IP laws based on international practice and accede to the *Berne Convention* by predetermined deadlines. The *1992 MOU* evidenced a huge imbalance of mutual obligations with the U.S. setting standards and China abiding by the rules (See Table 5.1.below).

Such a relationship illustrates Marxists' "relations of production" in the concept of "base and superstructure" (Storey, 2001, p. 83) which install one party as the dominating force and the other as the dominated. That is, the social force that controls materials of production takes the leading role in the relations of production (Storey, 2001, p. 83) while the opposite party is the subordinate. Critics adopting Marxist approach identify and interpret such relationships embodied in the texts in their historical context (Foss, 2004). For the purpose of this study, I mainly focus on Article 3 of the *1992 MOU* which deals solely with copyright to explore the relationship after I briefly summarize the agreement.

The 1992 conflict represents the initial formal U.S.-China debate over China's copyright/intellectual property right protection issue. It occurred at the beginning of the 1990s when China was not yet a member of the *Berne Convention*. The U.S. complained about copyright infringing in China in the *Special 301 Reports* (1989~2011), attributing the issue mainly to the inadequacies of China's copyright law and implementation regulations. The *1992 MOU* devotes most of its space to China's obligations while briefly mentioning U.S. duties, indicating an obviously imbalanced relationship between the two parties (See Table 5. 1.below). China's obligations included adjusting its intellectual property right legislation to international practice and acceding to international conventions which demonstrated the tremendous pressure China faced during the conflict settlement (See Table 5.1. below).

The *1992 MOU* first starts with a brief preamble that identifies the goal of the agreement: to maintain "the spirit of cooperation embodied in the bilateral Agreement of Trade Relations and consistent with the principles of the relevant international agreement" (the *1992 MOU*). Consisting of seven articles, the *MOU* deals with bringing China's patent law in line with the *Paris Convention* (Articles 1 & 2), copyright legislative changes to comply with the *Berne Convention* (Article 3) which I will discuss more in the following paragraph. It also emphasizes China's protection of trade secrets in industry (Article 4), mutual obligations of both governments to provide effective procedures, remedies, consultations on matters relating to protection, enforcement, obstacles of legitimate trade (Articles 5 & 6), and termination of Special 301 investigations and trade sanctions.

Article 3 of the *1992 MOU* is China's response to the conditions the U.S. bargained with to settle the copyright issue. China accepted each condition, ranging from addressing the inconsistencies of China's copyright law to changing China's non-member status which the U.S. believed to have contributed to rampant violations of the U.S. copyrights (*USTR Special 301 Reports*, 1989~2011). The section starts with China's promise to accede to the *Berne Convention*:

> The Chinese government will accede to the Berne Convention ... [by] submit[ting] a bill authorizing accession ... by April 1, 1992 ... enact the authorization of bill by June 30, 1992, ... [and then submit] its instrument of accession to the Berne Convention to the World Intellectual Property Organization to be effective by October 15, 1992. (the *1992 MOU*, Clause One)

The Chinese government must also accede to the *Geneva Convention* for the protection of phonographic products. Similarly, China will submit a bill to the legislative body by June 30, 1992 and enact it by February 1, 1993 (the *1992 MOU*, Clause Two).

Table 5. 1   **U.S.-China Copyright Conflict: Domination and Coercion versus Concessions and Negotiations**

Copyright Internationalization and Globalization as Represented by the *Convention* and the *TRIPS Agreement*	China's Obligations in the *1992 MOU* and *1995 IP Agreement* Concerning Copyright Protection	U.S. Obligations in the *1994 MOU* and *1995 IP Agreement* Concerning Copyright Protection

- National treatment - Minimum protection standard and duration - Developing country in conformity to international practice	- Accede to international copyright laws - Revise copyright laws and implementation regulations - Keep consistencies with the *Berne Convention* and the *MOU* when inconsistencies exist - Identify the status of the Convention in domestic laws - Inform their judicial and administrative bodies for enforcement purposes - Recognize computer programs as literary works, sounding recordings, and works not in the public domain - Protect US products (including computer programs and sound recordings)	- Indicate the status of the Conventions in their respective laws - Inform their judicial and administrative bodies for enforcement purposes - Protect Chinese works that meet "eligibility for protection" based on China's commitment
- More provisions added based on the *Berne Convention* - Minimum standards of protection by members - Enforcement provisions through domestic procedures and remedies	- Use copyright verification system and identifier - Protect digital products and motion pictures - Provide more market access for US copyrighted products and individuals and entities engaged in producing copyrighted products and materials - Publish laws, rules, regulations, guidance etc. to protect public morals/maintain social order - Exchange information and provide consultation	- Assist China in personnel training of skills in identifying and verifying infringing merchandise and lab testing as well as provide equipment - Exchange information and provide consultation - Terminate investigations and rescind retaliations

The U.S. demand for China to keep in line with international copyright practice does not limit to copyright revisions or the accessions to the two international conventions. It also stipulates that China should connect these international treaties to its civil code: when inconsistencies in civil code exist, international treatises prevail (the *1992 MOU*, Article 3, Clause 3). More importantly, China must "issue new regulations to comply with these conventions and the *MOU* by October 1, 1992" (the *1992 MOU*, Article 3, Clauses 3 & 4), which clarifies and explains "the exclusive right of distribution that applies to all works and sound recordings" (the *1992 MOU*, Article 3, Clause 3 & 4). The regulations apply to works by authors of the convention members as well as works created in contractual relationships, joint ventures, and commission from foreign capital and cooperative enterprises. In addition, Clause 4 rules that the Chinese government will submit a bill to amend its copyright law and enact the new version and the implementation regulations within a reasonable period (the *1992 MOU*, Article 3, Clause 3 & 4).

Clause 5 is concerned about mutual responsibilities for both governments. These responsibilities require the two sides to indicate the status of the conventions in their respective laws and inform their judicial and administrative bodies for enforcement purposes within 30 days after China's accession to the conventions and the signing of the *1992 MOU*.

In addition, the Chinese government was also required to recognize computer programs as literary works and sound recordings are also protected. Article 3 particularly stresses the protection of U.S. works which include computer programs and sound recordings published outside of China under the *1992 MOU* before China acceded to the Convention (Article 3, Clauses 6, 7, 8, and 9).

Compared to the strong emphasis of Chinese responsibilities, Article 3 only briefly mentions at the end that the U.S. will provide copyright protection for Chinese nationals based on two conditions: China is committed to the *MOU* and the works to be protected meet eligibility for protection (Article 3, Clause 9):

> Based on the commitments set forth in this MOU, the U.S. Government will take the necessary steps to secure to Chinese nationals and their works eligibility for protection under the copyright law of the United States which shall become effective no later than 60 days after signature of this MOU.

As is illustrated in the *1992 MOU*, the U.S. promoted internationalization of intellectual property rights protection in China, copyright in particular, by making China join the Conventions and adjust its copyright law and regulations to the international practice by predetermined dates. China would face trade sanctions if changes were not made. The *1992 MOU* reveals an imbalanced relationship in which the U.S. imposed regulations that China was to abide by them. A Marxist rhetorical approach maintains that this type of relations is closely connected with the "force of production" (Storey, 1998, p. 187) that the rivaling parties have at its disposal. The U.S. obviously had a much stronger "force of production" or "means of material production" (Marx and Engels, 1970, pp. 64-66) than China with its unparallel political, economic, military, and technological power that supports its unparalleled dominance in "the relations of production" (Storey, 1998, p. 187) of the treatise.

As a developing country at that point that had just started its market economic experiment and opened its door to the West, China was far from being able to challenge U.S. domination in terms of "forces of production" (Storey, 1998, p. 187). In addition, China was not yet a member of the WTO and had just established its copyright law which was still inconsistent with international conventions. Naturally, China had to accept subordination and made adjustment, particularly when it was increasingly dependent on the U.S. market for its export goods and U.S. technologies that often involve intellectual property rights (U.S. Census Bureau statistics).

To conclude, the findings in the *1992 MOU* clearly indicated that the agreement is a one-sided treatise in which the initiative rested with the U.S. who took complete control over the settlement and standard setting. Having more experience in copyright/intellectual property right legislation and protection as well as stronger economy and technologies, the U.S. was able to pressure China with threats of investigations and trade sanctions. China, on the contrary, was inexperienced in copyright legislation, had inconsistencies in its copyright law and regulations, had a great need for the U. S. advanced technologies, and relied on the U.S. market for its export goods. Therefore, China had to respond cooperatively and yield to the conditions the U.S. proposed (See Table 5.1. below). The reason behind the domination and concession is obvious: the U.S. had stronger material force that gave it a dominant position in the conflict settlement while China yielded to the conditions because it could not afford the potential harms of trade sanctions and Special 310 investigations.

5.3.2 China-United States Agreement Regarding Intellectual Property Rights (The *1995 IP Agreement*)

The signing of the *1995 U.S.-China IP Agreement* was a symbolic success for the U.S. It enhanced the *1992 MOU* by adding specific and long-term enforcement action plans and tasks and achieved larger access to the Chinese market for U.S. individuals and entities that engage in copyright production. The success secured more trade interests for the U.S. in the most populous and fast growing economy in the world. Moreover, it advanced the rule of law, disseminated the concept of equality, and supported individual achievement that reflected Western/U.S. rhetorical traditions and cultural values and beliefs through the U.S. participation in China's intellectual property practice.

On the contrary, Chinese rhetorical traditions and cultural values and beliefs tend to neglect the significance of formal legal enforcement. Such an approach to the law again produced the clash in copyright practice/IPR protection. As a result, China made tremendous concessions in the *1995 IP Agreement* to establish specific long and short term enforcement action plans and tasks under the U.S. pressure for fear of potential trade sanctions, loss of U.S. market for its export goods and barrier of importing advanced technologies. In doing so, China also subscribed to the U.S. values and beliefs. The conflict settlement involved domination, concession, coercion, and negotiation, elements that the Marxist rhetoric approach views as features of hegemony in texts and events. Therefore, in the following presentation, I first set forth the context by briefly introducing the background of the debate. I then adopt the approach of neo-Gramsci notion of hegemony to analyze the conflict settlement. In the analysis, I emphasize obligations of both sides in the agreement similarly as I did the *1992 MOU*. Lastly, I compare and contrast the implications of the conflict for the U.S. and Chinese copyright approaches.

The 1995 debate began two years after the *1992 MOU* was issued. The U.S. companies started to complain again about China's ineffective IP protection, claiming that China's failure to effectively protect U.S. IPRs caused an annual loss of over $800 million (Kanchuriak, 1994). The U.S. government promptly responded to the complaint. On June 30, 1994, USTR escalated its level of scrutiny of China's IP issue by once again moving China from the "priority watch list" to a "priority foreign country" followed immediately by Special 301 investigations (*USTR 301 Report*, 1989~2011). By December 31, after a six-month period was designated to negotiate the conflict, the two countries were still not able to reach an agreement. The U.S. government extended the period for sixty more days and announced 100% tariffs on over $1 billion worth of Chinese import products if an agreement could not be reached (Yu, 2002). While the Chinese government responded to the U.S. with same amount of retaliation on the American export goods as well as asserted that U.S. strategy would impact its automakers' possible future operations in China (Yu, 2002), hours before the deadline on February 26, 1995, the two parties reached the agreement with ample evidence that China again made tremendous concessions seemingly under U.S. pressure.

The *Agreement* is comprised of a letter from the Chinese minister of Foreign Trade and Economic Cooperation to Ambassador

Mickey Kantor, the then USTR head, and the Action Plan for Effective Enforcement of IPRs (Action Plan). The Agreement Letter (pp. 883-886) addresses China's efforts to improve IP protection through judicial and administrative procedures as well as enforcement actions, indicating China's determination/the U. S. pressure on China to profoundly improve its IPR environment. Judicially, the Chinese government has established specialized IP courts to handle infringement issues, such as stopping piracy, preserving property and evidence for effective litigation, and ordering compensation. Administratively, the State Council has set up the IPR protection structure and the Working Conference to take actions immediately. In terms of enforcement on copyright protection, China has taken effective actions. It has closed quite a few of factories that engaged in infringing, confiscated unauthorized products, and provoked business licenses of these factories. China will continue the effort to investigate suspected infringers.

The Action Plan offers specific enforcement actions and plans. Stressing IPRs enforcement structure and literacy campaigns, it highlights establishing state and sub-central working conferences, enforcement task forces and special enforcement period and efforts, enforcement through administrative agencies and departments, copyright verification systems, nationwide training and education, media obligations, and publication of laws (pp. 877-905). While the Action Plan covers all the primary types of IPRs, that is, patent, trademark, and copyright, it details what copyrighted products are protected and type of protection methods will be used. In addition, it gives more market access for U.S. copyrighted products and individuals and entities that produce copyrighted products and materials.

To explore the *1995 IP Agreement* using the Gramsci notion of hegemony (1971), the critic should take into account Gramsci's criteria when examining a rhetorical artifact. Gramsci's first criterion is "the supremacy of a social group manifests itself in [the way of] domination" (1971, p. 57). This is more than obvious in the case of the U.S.-China conflict of 1994~1995 that produced the *1995 IP Agreement*. For instance, my data indicated that in the aspect of China's copyright enforcement, the U.S. controlled standard setting completely as it succeeded in forcing China to take many enforcement measures and tasks which include:

- Establishing central and sub-central Working Conferences to coordinate, monitor, instruct, ensure, and direct protection measure, plans, tasks, and activities (the *1995 IP Agreement*, p. 887)
- Using copyright verification systems and unique identifier on CDs, CD-ROMs, and LDs, as well as motion picture products "to prevent the production of infringing goods and export of those goods" (the *1995 IP Agreement*, p. 883, 892).
- Setting up special enforcement period and actions (investigations and punishment)
- Planning multiple enforcement efforts in the fields of audio-visual products, motion pictures, computer programs, books and periodicals and other published materials (the *1995 IP Agreement*, pp. 893-895)

China has made some major enforcement efforts and will continue to do so to improve its copyright/IPRs protection. These task plans and actions resonate with the approach and goals of the *TRIPS Agreement* that strengthens and globalizes IPR protection and practice. In the U.S.-China conflicts, the U.S. as the most aggressive advocate of global IP practice was able to play the dominant role. The findings indicated that China was forced to make constructive and profound enforcement task plans and actions while the U.S. government had much less obligations which included providing personnel training and equipment (See Table 5. 1. above).

The second criterion in the Gramsci notion of hegemony is the supremacy of a social group that manifests itself in its "intellectual and moral leadership" (Gramsci, 1971, p. 57). By "leading" intellectually and morally, Gramsci was saying that the powerful (class) not only leads its allies (1971, p. 57) but also "dominates those who are its enemies" (p. 57) in promoting a certain cause that it justifies. He added that for a class or group that leads, "even before attaining power ... [it] can (and must) 'lead'; when it is in power it becomes dominant, but continues to 'lead' as well" (1971, p. 57). Situating the U.S.-China conflicts in its larger historical context will reveal the leadership role of the U.S. Further research indicated that the U.S. has been playing the leading role before, during, and after the establishment of the *TRIPS Agreement*. This leadership exhibits itself in the U.S. unrivaled powers in the political, economic, military, and technological fields, its achievement in gaining group consensus at the GATT conferences from countries that willingly identified with the U.S., using its domestic law effectively, the *Special 301 Report* to secure protection of the U.S. trade-related IPRs outside of the U.S., as well as gaining more market access through coercive strategies (Sell, 1995; Drahos, 2000).

The *1995 IP Agreement* indicated that the U.S. continued to play the dominant role in the conflict settlement and reaped greater achievement. While the *1992 MOU* succeeded in making China amend its copyright laws and implementation regulations and become conformed to international practice by joining the *Berne Convention*, the *1995 IP Agreement* complemented the *MOU* with intensive enforcement actions and plans. In addition, the U.S. was able to achieve more market access in China for its IP products and secured a sustaining role in China's copyright practice (See Table 5. 1).

In the *1995 IP Agreement*, China was forced to establish enforcement structures at both state and provincial levels and adopt copyright verification system, as well as use unique identifiers to prevent unauthorized products from being exported at the border. China was also made to initiate public campaigns and use mass media to increase public awareness of copyright protection. The more significant breakthrough the U.S. made in the settlement was China's promise of more market access for U.S. individuals and entities that engaged in producing audio-visual products such as CDs, DVDs, CD-ROMs, motion pictures, and printed materials. It is worth mentioning that ever since the early 1990s, the conflict never ends. It continues to be a major trade issue in U.S.-China bilateral trade relations and each time, China was under the USTR investigations and was even submitted to WTO for settlement (Morrison, 2011; Xinhua, 2011).

My findings indicated that in the conflict settlement, the U.S. was able to promote its idea of globalizing copyright practice in a foreign country. Gramsci's concept of hegemony is thus exemplified in the case for two reasons. First, the U.S. took an absolute control over the settlement and protection standard establishment as presented in previous discussions. Second, the U.S. was able to promote its objectives, ideals, values and beliefs, etc. by applying the *TRIPS Agreement* in settling trade-related IPRs issues in China. In addition, China was also required to launch trainings and public campaigns nationwide not only to educate enforcement personnel but also raise public awareness of copyright practice. Embedded in the enforcement plans and tasks, as well as the trainings and campaigns are Western ideas of universal rule of laws and level playing fields for individuals, and individual private ownership. Consequently, the U.S. moral and intellectual leadership expressed itself in its forcing China to bring copyright laws into conformity to international practice, enforce intensive enforcement plans and actions, and allow more market access for U.S. individuals and entities engaging in producing copyrighted products.

5.4 The Ideology of the Conflict: Implications for the U. S. and Chinese Copyright Approaches

The U.S.-China copyright conflict took place in the development of world copyright/IP practice that evolved from internationalization and globalization. It represents an ideological encounter between counter-interest groups of disproportional power in its settlement and standard setting, illustrating quite different perspectives of copyright practice and may result in different response to the settlement.

The U.S. and China have different experiences with copyright practice. When the conflict took place, the U.S. had been a strong advocate of copyright protection for a long time while China had just started the practice. China was still new in the field of IPR protection. China had primitive copyright laws in the beginning of the 20th century (Li, 2006; "The Dust-laden History Revisited...", 2011), but none of them had an effective effect on China's copyright protection due to constant political instabilities from 1900s to late 1940s: the dethroning of the Qing Dynasty in 1911, endless wars among warlords in 1920s, Japanese occupation from the 1930s to 1945, and civil war from 1946 to 1949. The Communist Party of China took power in 1949 and started to adopt state and collective ownership following the model of the Soviet Union. Until late 1970s, China was an orthodox socialism country applying planned economy. Therefore, an environment that encourages individual artistic and literary creations as well as stimulates the development of public welfare in the form of copyright protection did not exist. Individual writers and creators received a small fee for as rewards because all the works and innovations belonged to the people (country).

The first sophisticated copyright law was not issued until 1990 after China had changed its policy from seclusion to opening its door to the Western world for capitalist market economy. However, it did not join the *Berne Convention* until 1992 when the U.S. and China went into conflict over China's copyright/IP protection and China was required to accede to the *Berne Convention* in the *1992 MOU*.

Contrary to China's lack of real copyright legislation until 1990 and experience in protection, the U.S. had been practicing copyright protection within its borders for more than two hundred years since 1790 when the conflict took place. By then, the U.S. had joined the

Berne Convention for about three years and quickly secured great extent of leadership in international IP practice. Actually, the U.S. has carried the British common law tradition in the aspect of copyright protection from the beginning when the country was established. It perceives copyright protection a federal undertaking and believes it enhances scientific and artistic creations: "To promote the Progress of Science and useful Arts, by securing for limited Times to Authors and Inventors the exclusive Right to their respective Writings and Discoveries" (*U.S. Constitution*, Article 1, Section 8). "The U.S.A Copyright Act of 1790 ... granted copyright protection to citizens and residents of the U.S.A. This form of national protectionism prevailed in U.S. copyright policy for a surprising long period" although it "denied copyright protection to published works by foreigners, applying the 'nationality-of-the author' principle" (Drahos, 1998).

The U.S. began to exercise real leadership in international IP practice after WWII, particularly when it succeeded in lobbying for the connection between world trade and IPRs. Domestically, its copyright act has been revised to provide increasing benefits for the writers, creators, and copyright holders, such as extending term of protection. Beyond its borders, the U.S. first brought IPR protection to its trade law in 1970s and launched the notorious *Special 301 Report* for the U.S. government to speculate any international trade barriers caused by the violation of U.S. IPRs on the part of its foreign trade partners (Pechman, 1998). Based on the report, the U.S. government will settle the issue through bilateral negotiations followed by possible trade retaliations or other punishment if the opponent fails to make changes and improvement just like the China case. The promulgation of the *TRIPS Agreement* was a real breakthrough the U.S. made in the history of world IP practice which globalized the practice and established the U.S. leading role in the field.

The two bilateral agreements that the U.S. and China reached in 1992 and 1995 exemplify the U.S. aggressiveness in promoting international and global copyright/IP practice. The U.S. was the tough negotiator as can be seen in both agreements. It succeeded in forcing China to accede to the international copyright conventions, revise its copyright law and implementations to comply with international practice, make strategic plans, launch proactive actions on infringers, and winning more access to the Chinese market for U.S copyrighted products. The U.S. achieved all that was desired. Therefore, regardless of the laxness of its incorporation into the international copyright regime and rejection of the protection of foreign copyrights, the U.S. has more awareness of IPR, understands the necessity and significance of securing the property rights for individuals and entities, and believes copyright protection enhances more creations and innovations which eventually provides more social welfare for the general public.

China's approach to copyright/IPRs indicated a lack of awareness of copyright protection from the general public. This is normal, because copyright law did not exist in Communist China until 1990 when China issued its first comprehensive copyright act. However, there were inconsistencies in the law because China was not a member of the *Berne Convention*. Consequently, the U.S. contributed piracy in China to the inconsistencies (*Special 301 Reports*, 1989~2011) and its non-member status, believing that after China became a member of the international conventions and brought its copyright law into conformity to international practice, the Chinese would abide by the law. However, protection was dissatisfying. Less than two years later, the U.S. again escalated China from "priority watch list" to the status of "priority foreign country" (*USTR Special 301 Report*, 1989~2011), launched simultaneous investigations, and threatened a billion dollar retaliation on Chinese products for substantial improvement of copyright/intellectual rights protection in the Chinese market.

Reasons that caused rampant piracy vary as have been discussed in Chapters Three and Four, but an ideological approach to the U.S.-China conflict indicated in the two agreements provided evidence that copyright practice was mostly forced upon China by external pressure because the concept of copyright/intellectual property rights and the protection are still new in Chinese culture. When the conflicts took place, China had just imported IPR practice from the West and begun to educate the public that copyrights were private properties entitled to right holders. This was difficult for a culture that has always prioritized sharing and inner-group interest over individual benefits and a country that maintains state and collective ownership as its economic systems. The intensive and detailed enforcement task plans and actions signify a lack of effective protection mechanism and a need of public awareness of individual IPRs. Although copyright law and implementation regulations already exist, they did not and will not secure satisfactory protection.

Compared with China, U.S. culture tends to have a stronger sense of copyright protection. This was indicated first in the *1992 MOU* when the U.S. complained about the inconsistencies in China's copyright law with international practice. They believed that once China had revised its copyright law and implementation regulations and maintained conformity to the international practice and acceded to the international copyright conventions, China would be able to enforce protection of copyrights. However, China's copyright reality failed to meet the U.S. expectations when the U.S. found copyright enforcement was an issue despite there was a comprehensive copyright law and the liabilities of being a member of the international conventions. This forced the U.S. to take more forceful actions on China, the result of which was the *1995 IP Agreement* which is a much longer agreement that stressed intense enforcement measures.

The enforcement actions and plans exemplify the fact that China lacked copyright protection mechanism and law enforcement in the market. They also suggest that the U.S. has more awareness of individual intellectual properties and stronger protection which are illustrated in the effort to improve China's copyright environment. The conflict indicated that China was facing a strong external pressure from the U.S. pertaining to copyright/intellectual property laws and protection when it signed the agreements. It may also imply that the Chinese public may not ready for strong copyright protection although the government agreements were there. Such unpreparedness supported my findings in the previous two chapters. Chinese rhetorical tradition and cultural values and beliefs tended to rely on self-moral cultivation to regulate individual behavior rather than formal laws. As Sell (1995) observed, developing countries faced so much pressure in intellectual property right protection legislation and enforcement, particularly under the *TRIPS Agreement* and U.S. Special 301 investigations and potential trade sanctions, they may sign agreements, but they also resist even at great cost of their economy.

5.5 Conclusion

In this chapter, I adopted the approach of Marxism (classical and the neo-Gramsci hegemony) in the analysis of the U.S.-China copyright debate in the early 1990s. I first introduced internationalization and globalization of international copyright practice to contextualize the U.S.-China copyright conflict that produced the *1992 MOU* and *1995 IP Agreement*, because Marxism requires rhetorical texts/artifacts to be examined in the historical moment of their production. I then studied the U.S.-China copyright conflict by giving a brief background and examining the two agreements. My findings indicated that in each case, the U.S. was in dominant control of the settlement and standard setting, had a strong awareness of and belief in individual intellectual private rights, and thus promoted aggressively universal copyright protection. On the contrary, China was dominated in both cases and was forced to make tremendous concessions to prevent potential trade sanctions and maintain smooth business cooperation. The concessions were illustrated in its compliance with international copyright/intellectual property right practice, enforcement actions and plans, as well as opening more of its market for U.S. copyrighted products. These enforcement actions and plans also had the connotation that there was a general lack of copyright awareness in Chinese culture.

The differences in the awareness of copyright protection may impact the two cultures' response to copyright laws and regulations.

For the Chinese that are new in the field of intellectual property rights protection, copyright laws do not guarantee effective enforcement. As a result, copyright acts may seem laws on paper and external pressure will not bring about expected results. The U.S., on the other hand, has a long history of copyright practice and thus, relies on copyright acts to protect individual intellectual property rights. Laws are universal for all individuals who cherish their personal success and law enforcement is the effective way to protect individual interests. Consequently, copyright protection was effective. In next chapter, which will be the last chapter of the dissertation, I will focus on results and discussions that will include a summary followed by a reflection on the results as well as recommendations and limitations of the study.

Chapter Six

Discussions and Conclusions

6.1 Introduction

This rhetorical study has addressed U.S. and Chinese approaches to copyright practice in the U.S.-China conflict over China's copyright issue. The problem caused by dissonance between the American expectations for a safe copyright/IP environment in China and the reality of inadequate legal enforcement informed this inquiry. To establish the context for this project, I used a multifaceted theoretical framework to review the existing relevant literature on factors that impact China's copyright enforcement. For example, the main theories used in data analysis were comparative rhetoric, intercultural rhetoric/communication, and Marxist/ideological criticism. These theories consent that mankind uses language to interpret their world and create knowledge, and at the same time, are impacted by interpretations and constructed knowledge. In other words, the theories that I adopted in the project maintain that human perspectives of the world are social constructions and human actions and behaviors (discursive and non-discursive) are responsive to what they have seen, heard, and learned.

Using meta-rhetorical approaches, I chose my artifacts from three domains in relation to copyright protection: early Western and Chinese rhetorical texts, U.S. and Chinese government and/legal documents, and bilateral treaties. The findings revealed that a culture's approach to copyright is complex and no single factor would suffice to interpret the collective behavior toward copyright practice. Therefore, to complement existing research in the field, this survey explored the possible impact of rhetorical traditions, cultural values and beliefs, as well as ideological influence on copyright practice. In this final chapter, I summarize and discuss the results of this rhetorical study in addition to implications and recommendations.

6.2 Summary of Research Results

6.2.1 Western and Chinese Perspectives of *Virtue/Ethos* and their Impact on U.S. and Chinese Legal (Copyright) Approaches

In the first set of selected texts that recorded Western/Chinese rhetorical practice, ancient Western (Greek and Roman) and Chinese philosophers and rhetoricians all held that individuals' sense of *virtue/ethos* regulates human conduct and constitutes an integral component in maintaining social harmony. The Western concept of *virtue/ethos* has a broad scope that includes Plato's *virtue, justice,* temperance, holiness, and courage, Aristotle's *practical wisdom, virtue, goodwill,* and Cicero's *universal knowledge* particularly of the awareness of *civil law*. Among the elements of *virtue/ethos*, Plato, Aristotle, and Cicero emphasized the function of *virtue/ethos* and legal awareness/sense of *justice* in shaping human actions and influencing societal order.

The Chinese interpreted *virtue/ethos* differently. Confucius believed *ren*, meaning benevolence, love, gentleness, kindness, etc., was the individuals' virtuous quality and the cultivation of which would improve and harmonize interpersonal relationships for collective interest and social order. He further proposed adopting *li*, rituals of the Zhou Dynasty as the code of conduct through rectifying names and observing cardinal relationships to develop human benevolent characters. The other Confucian, Mencius, stressed the virtuous character of rulers, holding that benevolent governance would realize social harmony. The Daoists refuted the Confucian notion of benevolence and rituals, viewing it a human intrusion of natural order. Instead, Lao Zi suggested following the law of nature, the *Way* in his term, by means of *wu wei* (inaction) and *bu zheng* (non-contention) to maintain social harmony.

A comparison of Western and Chinese views of *virtue/ethos* indicated a differing perspective. Western notion of *virtue/ethos*, represented primarily in the works by Plato, Aristotle, and Cicero, not only embodies legal conformity, but also resortes to formal laws for social order. However, both Confucianism and Daoism relied on individual virtuous characters to regulate social order and rejected formal laws. Consequently, the Western perspective of *virtue/ethos* tends to lead people to conform their behavior to legal requirements and respect individual rights. Contrarily, the Chinese view of the concept encourages individuals to cultivate moral qualities, sacrifice individual interests for the benefits of the superiors and the collective, as well as skepticism and refusal of formal laws. Such differences reflected in copyright approach will bring more public awareness of IPRs, less infringing behavior, and strong legal protection on in the U.S.

6.2.2 U.S.-Chinese Values and Beliefs, Cultural Dimensions, and the Impact on their Copyright Approaches

The second part of my data analysis examined values and beliefs from four separate significant documents, two from the U.S. and two from China, their association with three pairs of dichotomous cultural orientations which may affect the particular culture's perspective of legal practice including copyright approach. The U.S. values and beliefs reflected in the *Declaration of Independence* and the *Constitution of the United States of America* sent strong messages as liberty, justice, freedom, the pursuit of individual happiness, independence, equality, and rule of law, illustrating the cultural dimension of universalism that emphasizes universal values and rule of law for all humans. These common values and beliefs were set forth in the *Declaration of Independence* which charged the British king for his violation of the natural rights the colonies should be given and were stressed to be secured in the *U.S. Constitution*.

The core values and beliefs in the two documents also reveal the individualistic characteristics of U.S. culture which stresses the realization of personal goals in the aspects of the political, the economic, and the social. The founding fathers of the U.S. recognized and fought for the "inalienable rights" for each individuals to pursue "Life, Liberty and the pursuit of Happiness"(*The Declaration of Independence*) and promised to "secure the Blessings of Liberty" through "establish[ing] Justice, insure domestic Tranquility, provide for the common defense, [and] promote the general Welfare" (*The U.S. Constitution*).

Low power distance represents the third cultural orientation in the U.S. texts. the *Declaration of Independence* explicitly resists inequality and hierarchy, charging the British King with controlling the American colonies through his power and depriving the American settlers of their rights to life, liberty, and the pursuit of happiness. *The U.S. Constitution* emphasized the value of equal rights and elaborated on them, particularly in the Bill or Rights pertaining to political, economic, social freedoms, and equal legal treatment.

The other part of analysis in Chapter Four focused on Chinese values and beliefs portrayed in the *Constitution of the People's Republic of China* and *Deng Xiaoping's Southern Tour Speeches*. Research results found two particular values and beliefs that illustrated China's particularistic cultural orientation based on the Hampden-Turner and Trompenaars (2000) and Hofstede (2001) criteria–patriotism and socialism with Chinese characteristics that prioritizes allegiance and loyalty to the country or the ruling party and allows exceptions for people, situations, and events. For example, currently China is adopting socialism as its political system with one party ruling the country dictatorially. At the same time, it is practicing capitalist market economy. This complexity creates the uniqueness of China's current transition and has an impact on every aspect of Chinese life.

Research on those Chinese texts also found China has a stronger orientation of collectivism over individualism. *China's Constitution* and *Deng's Speeches* revealed some values and beliefs typical of collectivist cultures that emphasize patriotism/nationalism, state and collective ownership, and peace and harmony. *China's Constitution* keeps a lengthy preamble which functions as "patriotic education" for the general public that narrated China's contemporary history characterized by foreign invasions and domestic instabilities until the Communist took power in 1949. The purpose of this education is to honor China and the government ruled by the Communist Party. *Deng's Speeches* also addressed maintaining the state and collective ownership when he was reassuring his audience that capitalism constituted only a small part of China's economy.

My research results also found examples of high power distance in some of the values and beliefs. For example, politically, China maintains socialist system (with Chinese characteristics) which means one political party rules the country dictatorially and does not accept challenge of power from other political parties. Both *China's Constitution* and *Deng's Speeches* stressed maintaining the sole rule of the Communist Party of China (*Deng's Speeches*; *China's Constitution*, Preamble). From the economic aspect, China adopts state and collective ownership systems, indicating state and collective interests prioritize over individual private interests. From the family level, the *Constitution* explicitly decrees that children should pay filial respect for and take care of their elderly parents. High power distance that tolerates hierarchy and inequality of power distribution may have a negative impact on legal practice and copyright protection when individual private interest gets in the way of state and collective interest and the more powerful; power is likely to be abused.

A comparison and contrast of U.S. and Chinese values and beliefs revealed striking differences in cultural orientations which impact the two cultures' approach to legal practice such as copyright. The U.S. cultural dimensions of universalism, individualism, and low power distance that value rule of law for all, individual interest, and equal treatment may result in a strong sense of legal justice and protection of individual intellectual property rights. Chinese cultural preference in particularism, collectivism, and high power distance tends to allow rule of law by man, neglect of individual private properties, and abuse of law that cause more piracy and less effective copyright protection.

6.2.3 The U.S.-China Copyright Conflicts: Domination and Concessions as well as Implications

The third set of texts I examined were two bilateral intellectual property treatises, the *1992 MOU* and the *1995 IP Agreements*. Both agreements exemplified that the U.S. dominated the conflict settlement and standard setting of legislation revisions and enforcement actions and plans while China submitted to subordination, indicating an imbalanced relationship existed between the two parties. The 1992 Agreement aimed to internationalize IP practice in China, so its focus was mainly on inconsistencies in China's newly issued copyright law and implementation regulations and China's non-membership status. China was made to revise its IP laws and regulations to keep in line with international practice and accede to international copyright conventions.

The *1995 IP Agreement* bears influence of the *TRIPS Agreement* negotiated in 1994 that aims to globalize intellectual property practice, and therefore, focuses on enforcement. The U.S. achieved more control and China made more concessions to avoid a billion dollars worth of trade retaliation. China promised to launch intensive copyright enforcement plans and actions such as shutting down factories that had engaged in infringing and revoking their licenses, using copyright verification system and unique identifier to prevent pirated products from being exported, investigating suspicious and punishing infringers, establishing enforcement structures at both state and local levels, and initiating public campaigns for copyright awareness. Moreover, the U.S. gained more market access for individuals and entities engaged in producing or distributing copyrighted materials, such as CDs, DVDs, Computer programs, and CD-ROMs, databases, sound recording, and motion pictures. The U.S. achievements indicate China's submission to the pressure and domination.

The relationship between the U.S. and China formed in the conflict settlement and characterized by domination and concessions also indicates different approaches to copyright. While the U.S. was a strong advocate of copyright internationalization and globalization, China was still new with the field and therefore, lacked awareness of copyright as private properties and experience in the field of intellectual property right protection. Although sophisticated copyright law and implementation regulations are available and strong enforcement actions and plans are established under pressure, coercions, or willingly, it is very unlikely that China's copyright protection will dynamically change within a short time frame.

6.3 Conclusions

6.3.1 Outcome: The Rule of Law in Western/U.S Approach to Copyright Practice

Copyright practice, as a Western concept, embodies two implications: the protection of individual private property that connects with economic interest, intellectual integrity, and motivation for future creations and innovations as well as the consideration of public welfare through access to knowledge and technology. Therefore, the concept automatically secures that the owner has the exclusive limited right to distribute, print, and copy his/her literary or artistic property as soon as the work is created. Anyone else who uses the work in these ways must obtain permission (WIPO, "What is intellectual property?"; "Copyright Law of the United States of America"). Such an approach indicates a requirement of respect for and a strong legal protection of individuals' private IP which echoes the notion of *virtue/ethos* in Western rhetorical tradition, values and beliefs of U.S. cultural dimensions, and the aggressive ideological orientation in the effort to globalize copyright/IP practice.

Western rhetoricians primarily examined in the project all emphasized the importance of legal awareness in human virtuous qualities. Plato agreed that an individual's sense of *justice* is innate and can also be cultivated through learning and experience to regulate human behavior and social order. The lack of public consciousness of *justice* will cause disharmony of society (*Protagoras*, 357). Aristotle directly connected *justice*, the human virtuous quality with personal happiness that a lawful and democratic country provides. For instance, Aristotle maintained that such a society allows "individuals privately and all people generally" to pursue "happiness" that combine success with *virtue*. He described the happiness to be "self-sufficient in life ... accompanied with the ability to defend and use" "the abundance of possessions" (*On Rhetoric*, I. 5. 3). His concept of happiness refers to individuals' right to their possessions and the protection of such private properties through *justice*, laws, and democracy, the notion of lawfulness that exemplifies ancient Greek's approach to *virtue*, law and order, and individual interests (*On Rhetoric*, I. 13. 2; Prooemion, Kennedy, 1994; Reynolds, 1993). In addition, Aristotle associated *justice* with written law, recognizing its function in regulating individual behavior through legal enforcement (*On Rhetoric*, I. 9. 5). Cicero placed a significant value on the knowledge of public law for an *ideal orator*. He emphasizes that an *ideal orator* with such individual qualities will be persuasive in all rhetorical contexts and directs his audience to the right direction, and brings about a peaceful and tranquil nation (*De Oratore*, I. viii) where individuals have "a sense of fitting" (*De Oratore*, I. XLVI).

The ancient Greek and Roman concepts of *virtue/ethos* that emphasize *justice*, lawfulness, and individual rights are promoted and adjusted to special U.S. social context. U.S. culture cherishes freedom, independence, democracy, and human quality (the *U.S. Constitution*; the *Declaration of Independence*). Such values and beliefs require an equal legal treatment through the rule of law. For example, the *Declaration of Independence* petitions for a redress of the unjust treatment to the American colonies that were entitled to the rights of life, liberty, and the pursuit of happiness. The *U.S. Constitution* detailed specific individual rights through administrative, legislative, and judicial actions that include the respect and protection of intellectual property. Such a universalistic approach to legal practice and individualism privileges individuals' lawful rights to the cherishing of his/her personal achievements regardless of his political, economic, and social status.

Copyright internationalization and globalization, as well as U.S.-China conflict over China's copyright issue illustrate Western, particularly the U.S. ongoing effort to advocate the ideal of universal legal practice in global trade. It represents values of individualism and cherish of equal competition (May, 2002). As Bender concluded, copyright/intellectual property regime and its enforcement were established and promoted under modern capitalism and Western liberal thinking (2006). Consequently, it inherits "a characteristic value of the West in general and the U.S. particular" (Swineyard, Rinne, and Kauk, 1990) that assures "individual freedom and benefits are emphasized over social benefits" and "individual intellectual creative developments have individual ownership" (Swineyard, Rinne, and Kauk, 1990). To secure the right and benefit, the U.S. attempts to narrow the gap of copyright laws and protection among countries in the world (Mathur, 2003) and promotes its fundamental values of rule of law and level playing fields for competitions that see little relativity which challenges, and is challenged by China where a whole different culture exists.

6.3.2 Outcome: The Rule of Man in Chinese Approach to Copyright Practice

China's copyright protection is a new practice introduced from the West under international pressure, especially from the U.S. (Tang, 2004) that has only been taken seriously in the legislation for two decades (Cai, 2007). China has established a comprehensive copyright law and corresponding implementation regulations parallel to world-class copyright regime (Tian, 2007). However, "the sense of copyright in society as a whole is still somewhat hazy" (Tang, 2004) as indicated in the rampant piracy of copyrighted materials (Cai, 2007; Sell, 1995; Alford, 1995; Feng and Wei, 2002). This is because the emphasis of traditional Chinese culture on self-altruism over individual benefits, personal obligations rather than rights, as well as hierarchy that prioritizes personal status over law challenges the Western concept of the rule of law.

Both Confucians and Daoists preferred individual self cultivation of *virtue* and rejected formal legal practice, maintaining that laws regulate human behavior through punishment but fail to bring convinced compliance (*The Analects*; *Mencius*; *Dao De Jing*). I found that Confucius promoted human benevolence primarily by means of following the rituals established by sage kings in the past, proposing that ordering individuals in hierarchy would solve social problems: "To subdue one's self and return to propriety, is perfect virtue" and "when the prince is prince, and the minister is minister; when the father is father, and the son is son" (*The Analects*, 12; translated by Legge, 1891). Mencius enhanced Confucius' notions of benevolence and rituals, as well as the strategies to order society. However, he focused more on the benevolent quality of the rulers:

> Treat with the reverence due to age the elders in your own family, so that the elders in the families of others shall be similarly treated; treat with the kindness due to youth the young in your own family, so that the young in the families of others shall be similarly treated ... The kingdom [then] may be made to go around in your palm (*Mencius*, 2. 12).

Mencius believed that the "kindness of heart of a prince will suffice" (2. 12) to win the support from his people. Although Lao Zi identified *virtue* differently from Confucius and believed following natural law is the correct way and virtuous quality, he also emphasized individual self cultivation but through a differing path: in-action and non-contention. Lao Zi thus described the successful governance: "Therefore the sage, in the exercise of his government, empties their minds, fills their bellies, weakens their wills, and strengthens their bones" (*Dao De Jing*, 3). In doing so, the sages kept their people at rest. Here, Lao Zi proposed abstinence from desire and action for universal order of society. Such an approach to life rejects reliance on law whose functions are settling interpersonal conflict and maintaining social harmony.

The modern Chinese documents I examined carry the influence of China's ancient rhetorical tradition particularly in their emphasis on patriotism and loyalty to the ruling political party and the country, public interest over individual benefits, and hierarchy based on social status. Both *China's Constitution* and *Deng's Speeches* stress the dictatorial leadership of the Communist Party. The *Constitution* rationalizes the legitimate rule of the Communist Party by claiming that it was the Communist Party that accomplished China's democratic revolution by overthrowing "the rule of feudalism, imperialism, and bourgeois capitalism" (*China's Constitution*, Preamble). In addition, it emphasizes individuals' duty to safeguard the country and underlines reciprocal obligations of children and parents toward each other, as well as national harmony between all ethnic groups (*China's Constitution*, II. 4, 49, 52). The *Constitution* and *Deng's Speeches* both address collective interests through public ownership and common prosperity, reducing individual benefits to an insignificant position. Such values and beliefs tend to spawn man control due to power abuse and neglect of individual private rights caused by prioritizing collective interests. They run into conflict with Western/U.S. concept of copyright practice which identifies knowledge as private property and promotes its universal protection.

The U.S.-China debate over China's copyright issue reflects a conflict in values and beliefs that involves domination of one party and concession of the other. The U.S. represents the powerful, taking the leading role of copyright globalization with its strong capacity to generate and export technologies. China, with its short history of copyright practice, is not a match to the U.S. Having just established an extensive copyright law in 1990 and joined the *Berne Convention* in 1992 due to external pressure, the public that has been influenced by ancient and current rhetorical and cultural influences generally lacks the consciousness of individual intellectual property rights. Such inadequate awareness manifests itself in the many adjustments of copyright legislation and enforcement actions and plans as well as continuing widespread infringing of copyrighted materials (Mathur, 2005; Tang, 2007; Sell, 1995; Summar and Konan, 2002) which challenges the normality and hegemony of the West/U.S. system of IP system and practice (Parry, 2002).

6.4 Recommendations for the Discipline and Policy Makers

6.4.1 Rhetoric and Professional Communication: Research and Teaching

This study has addressed dynamic and complex contexts with multiple implications for different audiences. For example, in the field of rhetoric and professional communication, there are very few studies conducted on copyright/intellectual property practice across cultures, let alone using manifold comparative approaches. Projects such as this rhetorical exploration have significances in opening for imperative ways for comparative inquiries that address cultural differences in U.S.-China copyright/intellectual property practice as well as other cross-cultural communication contexts.

First, let me take this project as an example. The approach of comparing rhetorical traditions using early artifacts allows researchers in the field to trace back in-depth how ancient rhetoricians shaped and influenced a culture's thinking and decision making through language use pertaining to the culture's perspective of copyright practice. In my study, I found both ancient Western and Chinese rhetoricians stressed the importance of individual virtuous qualities such as *virtue/ethos* and an ideal orator's *knowledge of public law,* as well as *ren, li,* and *dao,* but they understood these qualities differently. The Greek and Roman rhetoricians attached legal compliance to individuals' virtuous quality and recognized the vital influence of formal laws in regulating behavior and maintaining social justice and democracy. The Chinese rhetoricians tended to rely solely on individual moral awareness to restore social harmony.

In addition, intercultural rhetoric/communication facilitates a better understanding of cultural values and beliefs that carry the influence of rhetorical tradition as well as explains a culture's decision making in different communication contexts. In working on the project, I found it an effective and appropriate way to study U.S. and Chinese cultural dimensions which have influenced the two cultures' perspectives of individual private property such as copyright.

Also, ideological criticism using bilateral copyright/IP agreements made it possible for me to explain the U.S.-China copyright debate that reflects rhetorical and cultural influences. Using this method, I was able to analyze the two cultures' ideological encounter in the movement of copyright/IP internationalization and globalization.

I view my effort as a preliminary research that attempted a comparative investigation of copyright approaches of the U.S. and China through a rhetorical perspective. I extended Kennedy's (1998) objectives of comparative rhetorical method by identifying key notions in rhetorical (and cultural) texts and applied what I have learned into cross-cultural communication in the context of global copyright practice. I also added an ideological perspective by looking into U.S.-China copyright conflict that took place in the background of the movement of copyright/IP internationalization and globalization. Nevertheless, future researchers can accomplish much more. While this research included only U.S. and Chinese rhetorical and cultural traditions and was limited to the topic of copyright approaches, they could choose either other cultures or multiple cultures of their interest for potential investigations and study different communication situations. They could also use this approach to examine subcultures in the U.S. Such efforts will broaden the scope of knowledge in our field and enhance cultural understandings in communication.

Secondly, instructions that introduce such meta-approaches in the rhetoric and professional communication classes will benefit our students. Obviously, there is a lack of intercultural rhetoric instruction in our field when many other programs in the humanities are providing information pertaining to history, languages, literature, and philosophy of other cultures. That to know others will help us know ourselves better is my adaptation and translation of the famous saying in the book of *The Art of War* (3. 6) by Sun Tze (544 B.C.E~496 B.C.E) who is recognized as a strategist and philosopher both in China and the West. I make this recommendation because there is a need in our field to bring more informed scholarship of current research and knowledge to the classroom. Increasing exchanges in all fields of life between the two countries call for this endeavor. Take trade communication as an example. China ranks the second top U.S. trading partner after Canada (U.S. Census Bureau, 2011). At the same time, conflicts will continue. Therefore, better understanding of cultural issues will improve mutual understanding. It is also because communication with cultures other than our own increases faster than any time in human history when technology changes the world into a "village". A better knowledge of values and beliefs and their impact on communication across cultures prepares our students to be more informed communicators in their future life and career.

6.4.2 U.S. and Chinese Policy Makers

The research also offers an opportunity for U.S. policy makers to revisit their rationales and insistence on their current policies toward China's copyright/IP protection. For example, current U.S. policies for dealing with China's copyright issue have been focusing on coercions and have not achieved expected results. These policies have misled the U.S. public into believing that China's copyright piracy is the biggest threat to U.S. companies of high copyright profiles and the situation is exacerbated by politicians attempting for more votes (Shwabach, 2008). Many researchers have addressed their concerns about the negative result of coercive strategies that hegemonize information and technology (Drahos, 1995; Sell, 1995; Shwabach, 2008). For example, Sell (1995) believed coercions cause resistance from developing countries and explained the reason why intellectual property infringing becomes a universal issue. Drahos proposed recommendations for developing countries to voice their interest in intellectual property practice in world trade (2002).

In his study of U.S.-China intellectual property debate, Shwabach (2008, pp. 73-74) examined a study commissioned by the Motion Picture Association (MPA) in 2006. The research reported that while piracy in the U.S. domestic market caused biggest loss ($1,300 million) to the U.S. movie industry, "the three other countries in which the losses to U.S. studios were highest were two developed countries (the U.K. and France: $406 million and $322 million) and one developing country (Mexico: $483 million). China ranked Number Six ($244 million) after Russia ($266) and Spain ($253) while closely followed by Japan, Italy, and Germany ($216 million,

$161 million, and $157 million). Shwabach (2008, p. 75) also found out from the report that while China takes the top spot "by total amount of consumer spending lost to piracy rather than just piracy of MPA members' IP ($2689 million), China's per capita piracy rate is the lowest among the ten countries examined (population in millions: 1,299; loss per capita; $2.07). He resonated with Drahos and Sell's unanimous perspective of the U.S.'s unfair treatment of China in terms of China's piracy of U.S. movie products. He thus concluded that such insistence on harsh enforcement of IP rights arouses:

> ...an intensity of resentment [when] people have been apparently sentenced to death in the name of U.S. IP interest (quoted in Alford, 1995)... and unhappy echoes of the colonial era, when the European and Japanese colonists' onslaught of the nineteenth and early twentieth centuries ... saw the country's sovereignty and property handed over bit by bit to foreigners and which China barely survived as a nation. Many in China see the penalties imposed on IP pirates as a sacrifice made by their government to appease the U.S. (2008, p. 76)

A more reasonable solution to the issue might be education in combination with legal enforcement. After all, China needs more time to cultivate public awareness of IPRs (Wang, 2004; Tang, 2004; Cai, 2007; Zhu, 2004) like the U.S. once did when it took more than one hundred years for the country before it started to protect foreign copyrights after rampant infringing of European literary works.

Similarly, Chinese policy makers should also reexamine China's copyright issue that constantly presents obstacles to the country's globalization process when concerns of copyright/IP protection are raised and shadow over Sino-U.S. relations. China began to practice economic reform more than thirty years ago with the ambitious goal to bring modernization to the country in the fields of agriculture, industry, national defense, and science and technology. China also understands that the goal would be a mission impossible if the country does not globalize its economy by adapting to corresponding international practice, such as the *Berne Convention* and the *TRIPS Agreement* that I previously described. Therefore, many laws were established between 1980s and 1990s which include copyright laws and implementation regulations. However, sophisticated laws do not guarantee effective protection as indicated by China's low IPRs index (5.5) as opposed to the much higher ranking of developed countries' indexes which range from 7.5 to 8. 5 (Jackson, 2011).

In addition, ineffective copyright/IPR protection constantly causes conflicts and potential trade wars between China and the United States. For example, for the past twenty more years, China has been regularly placed on USTR's "priority watch list" (*USTR Special 301 Reports*, 1990~2010). Each conflict resulted in lengthy negotiations, speculations of the U.S. government, criticism from other developed countries, and trade concessions such as the two cases discussed earlier.

While I recommend U.S. policy makers to consider local factors regarding the complexity of China's copyright practice and exercise patience and allow more time for a gradual change, I strongly advocate that China should improve its enforcement to seriously take into account global practice. More specifically, the government needs to strengthen enforcement and develop sustaining copyright/IP awareness programs for the general public. In doing so, the two countries may expect to find effective bilateral communication beneficial for both countries.

6.5 Limitations of the Study

Like all researches, this investigation has its own limitations. After I have identified the issue for the study, formulated my research questions, and designed appropriate methods to explore answers to the inquiries, I encounter two particular issues in the process that deserve to be mentioned: dependency on U.S. researches and a lack of study by colleagues in the field of rhetoric and professional communication.

The first limitation is the project's dependency on U.S. researches on China's copyright/IP issue that mainly had a Western perspective which could create bias for a comparative study. For instance, in the introductory chapter where I reviewed current literature on the U.S-China copyright conflict, I found the majority of the studies were conducted by U.S. researchers while most of the rest non-U.S. scholars are either situated in Europe or have been educated in the West that includes the U.S. who naturally tend to be influenced by Western/U.S. perspectives. In addition, there was very limited access to corresponding Chinese studies. The reasons might be (1) the U.S. is a strong advocate of copyright globalization and therefore, the topic attracts more attention from scholars in the country. (2) U.S. libraries do not have an abundant depository of Chinese studies on U.S.-China copyright conflict. (3) The Internet does not provide much free access to Chinese scholarly sources.

The lack of study on world copyright/IP practice in the field of rhetoric and professional communication represents the other limitation. Although I take this gap positively and view it as an opportunity for me to open up a conversation, I do believe it would be beneficial to have established knowledge on the topic from other peer colleagues.

To bridge the disparity caused by dependency on researches of the Western perspective and lack of resources from our field, I emphasized the artifacts themselves, believing that a textual analysis presents a genuine look of the issue in question.

6.6 Contributions

This study presents a preliminary effort to compare and contrast Western/U.S. and Chinese rhetorical and cultural traditions and their impact on the two cultures' approaches to copyright practice. It adds to the corpus of knowledge about U.S.-China conflict over copyright/IP protection and possible communication issues in other areas between and beyond the two countries. Using a rhetorical perspective, this study is also an initiative endeavor that brings the lens of rhetoric to the specific communication context of global copyright/IP practice in different countries that few have explored. It serves my major purposes of increasing cultural awareness in different communication situations and broadening the scope of research and practice in rhetoric and professional communication.

References

Agreement on Trade-Related Aspects Of Intellectual Property Rights. (1994). *Retrieved August* 10, 2009, from WTO Web site: http://www.wto.org/english/tratop_e/trips_e/t_agm0_e.htm.

Alford, W. (1999). A Second Great Wall? China's Post-Cultural Revolution Project of legal Construction. *Cultural Dynamics, 11* (7), 193-213.

---. (2002). Of Lawyers Lost and Found: Searching for Legal Professionalism in the People's Republic of China. In L. C. Arthur Rosett (Ed.). *East Asian Law and Development: Universal Norms and Local Culture.* New York: RoutledgeCurzon.

---. (1995). *To Steal a Book Is an elegent Offense: Intellectual property Law in Chinese Civilization.* Stanford: Stanford University Press.

American Society of International Law (1995). *China-United States: Agreement Regarding Intellectual Property Right.* Washington: International Legal Materials.

Aristotle. (1991). *On Rhetoric: A Civic Discourse.* G. A. Kennedy (Trans.). Oxford: Oxford University Press.

Beamer, I. and Varner, L. (2001). *Intercultural Communication in the Global Workplace.* Boston: McGraw-Hill.

Berne Convention for the Protection of Literary and Artistic Works. (1886). Retrieved August 1, 2009, from WIPO Web site: http://www.wipo.int/treaties/en/ip/berne/trtdocs_wo001.html.

Berrell, M. and Wrathall, J. (2007). Between Chinese Culture and the Rule of Law. Management Research News, 30 (1), pp. 57-76.

Bettig, R. V. (1996). *Copyrighting Culture : the Political Economy of Intellectual Property.* Boulder: Westview Press.

Bizzell, P. (2001). *The Rhetorical Tradition: Reading from Classical Times to the Present.* Boston: Bedford/St. Martin's.

Bogdan, R. C. and Biklen, A. K. (2003). *Qualitative Research for Education: An Introduction of Theories and Methods.*

Braithwaite, J. and Drahos, P. (2000). *Global Business Regulations.* Cambridge: Cambridge University Press.

Bransetetter, L. F. (2006). Do Stronger Intellectual Property Rights Increase international technology Transfer? Empirical Evidence from U. S. Firm-Level Panel Data. *The Quarterly Journal of Economics, 121* (1), pp. 321-349.

Burke, K. (1950). *A rhetoric of motives.* Berkeley: University of California Press.

Burke, K. (1931). *Counter-Statement.* Los Angeles: Herms Publications.

Burke, K. (1966). *Language as Symbolic Action.* Berkeley: University of California Press.

Cai, D. J. (1999). Development of the Chinese legal System Since 1979 and Its Current Crisis and Transformation. *Cultural*

Dynamics, *11* (2), 135-166.

Cai, X.Q. (2006). *Lao Zi Shuo/Lao Zi Says*. Wang, Q, Jiang, F. Z(Trans.). Beijing: Chinese Language Education Press.

Cao, D. (2004). *Chinese Law: A Language Perspective*. Aldrshot: Ashgate Publishing.

Cai, F. H. (2007, October 23). *Intellectual Property Protection: a Public Perspective*. Retrieved March 1, 2011, from People Net: http://finance.people.com.cn/GB/8215/59360/6462375.html.

Chinadaily. (2011, March 16). *The dust-laden History Revisited - the Story of the Copyright Code of Great Qing Dynasty*. Retrieved June 15, 2011, from China Intellectual Property: http://ipr.chinadaily.com.cn/2011-03/16/content_12181207.htm.

Cicero, M. T. (2001). *Cicero: On the Ideal Orator*. J. M. Wisse (Trans.). Oxford: Oxford University Press.

Collison, C. et. al. (2003, October 16). Core Democratic Values: Words to Live by. Retrieved March 1, 2011, from Michigan State website: www.michigan.gov/documents/nal-mnm-mnm-corevalues-wordstoliveby-pgz_76505_7_pdf.

Combs, S. (2006). *The Dao of Rhetoric*. New York: State University of New York Press.

Confucius. (211 B. C. E.). *The Analects*. J. Legge, (Trans.). New York: Dover Books. Retrieved August 10, 2009, from eBooks@Adelaide: http://ebooks.adelaide.edu.au/c/confucius/c748a/.

Constitution of the People's Republic of China. Retrieved August 10, 2009, from People's Daily Online Web site: http://english.peopledaily.com.cn/constitution/constitution.html.

Constitution of the United States. Retrieved August 10, 2009, from National Archives Web site: http://www.archives.gov/exhibits/charters/constitution.html.

Creswell, J. (2002). *Research Design: Qualitative, Quantitative, and Mixed Methods Approaches.* Thousand Oaks: Sage Publications Inc.

Deng, X. P. (1992). "Excerpts From Talks Given in Wuchang, Shenzhen, Zuhai, and Shanghai". Retrieved September 27, 2009, from the University of Mississippi Web site: http://www.olemiss.edu/courses/pol324/dengxp92.htm.

Drahos, P. (2002). Developing Countries and Internationalization of Intellectual Property Standard-setting. *The Journal of World Intellectual Property , 5* (5), pp. 765-789.

Drahos, P. (1995). Global property Rights in Ifnormation: The Story of TRIPS at the GATT. *Promethus , 16* (1), 6-19.

Drahos, P. (2007). *Information Feudalism: Who Owns the Knowledge Economy?* New York: The New Press.

Drahos, P. (1998). *The Universality of Intellectual Property: Origins and Development.* WIPO.

Edger A. and Sedgwick, P. (2002). *Cultural Theory: The Key Concepts.* New York: Routledge.

Education, M. D. (n.d.). *State of Michigan.* Retrieved October 15, 2010, from Our core Democratic values—State of Michigan: http://www.michigan.gov/documents/10-02_Core_democtaric_Values_48832_7.pdf.

Feder, G. S. (1996). Enforcement of Intellectual Property Rights in China: You Can Lead A Horse to Water, but you can't make it drink. *Virginia Journal of International Law Association , 37*, 223-.

Feng, X. Q. (2002). Internationalization of Copyright System and the 2001 Amendment of the Copyright Law of the People's Republic of China. *The Journal of World Intellectual Property, 5*

(5), 743-763.

Feng, X. and Wei, Y. (2002). Internationalization of the Copyright System and the 2001 Amendment of the Copyright Law of the People's Republic of China. *The Journal of World Intellectual Property*, *15* (5), 743-763.

Foss, S. K. (2004). *Rhetorical criticism: Exploration and practice*. Long Grove: Waveland Press Inc.

Ganea, P., Pattlon, T. and Heath, C. (Ed.). (2005). *Intellectual Property Law in China*. London: Kluwer Law International.

Ganea, P. P. (Ed.). (2005). *Intellectual Property Law in China*. London: Kluwer Law International.

Ghorra-Gobin, C. (2005, March). *Social and Human Sciences*. Retrieved May 15, 2009, from H-Net Reviews in the Humanities and Social Sciences: http://www.h-net.org/reviews/showpdf.php?id=10305.

Golden, J. B. (1983). *The Rhetoric of Western Thought*. Dubuque: Kendall Hunt Publishing.

Hall, D. E. (2001). *Literary and Cultural Theory*. Boston: Houghton Mifflin Company.

Hall, E. (1976). *Beyond culture*. New York: Anchor Books.

Hampden-Turner, C. M. and Trompenaars, F. (2000). Building Cross-Ccultural Competence: How to Create Wealth from Cconflicting Values. Yale: Yale University Press.

Herrick, J. (2005). *History and Theory of Rhetoric*. Boston: Allyn and Bacon.

Hofstede, G. (2001). *Culture's Consequences: Comparing Values, Behaviors,Institutions and Organizations Across Nations*. Thousand Oaks: Sage Publications Inc.

Holtz-Eakin, D. (2005). *Economic Relationships Between the United*

States and China. Washington D. C.: Congressional Budget Office.

Indepence Hall Association. (1995, July 4). *UShistory*. Retrieved October 1, 2010, from UShistory: http://www.ushistory.org/declaration/document/.

Intellectual Property Office. (2006). *A Brief History of Copyright*. Retrieved October 10, 2009, from IP Rights Office: http://www.iprightsoffice.org/copyright_history/.

Kachuriak, K. M. (1995). Copyright Piracy: Analysis of the Problem and Suggestions for Protection of U.S. Copyrights. *Dick. J. Int'l L*, *13*, 599.

Kennedy, G. A. (1994). *A New History of Classical Rhetoric*. Princeton: Princeton University Press.

Kennedy, G. A. (1997). *Comparative Rhetoric: An Historical and Cross-Cultural Introduction*. Oxford: Oxford University Press.

La Croix, S. J. and Konan, D. E. (2002). Intellectual Property Rights in China: The Changing Political Economy of Chinese-American Interests. *The World Economy, 25(6)*, 759-788.

Legge, J. (1891). *The Texts of Taoism*. New York: Dover Publications, 1962.

Legge, J. (1875). *The Life and Works of Mencius*. New York: Dover Publications, 1970. Retrieved August 2, 2009, from Internet Sacred Text Archive: http://www.sacred-texts.com/cfu/menc/.

Lu, X. (1998). *Rhetoric in Ancient China, fifth to third century B.C.E: A Comparison with Classical Greek Rhetoric*. Columbus: University of South Carolina.

Maskus, K. (1998). The Role of Intellectual Property Rights in Encouraging Foreign Direct Investment and Technology Transfer. *Duke J. of Comp. & Int'l L , 8*, 109-161.

Maskus, K. (2000). *Intellectual Property Rights in The Global Economy*. Washington: Peterson Institute.

Maskus, K. E., Dougherty, S. M. and Mertha, A. (2005). Intellectual Property Rights and Economic Development in China. In C. Fink and K. E. Maskus, *Intellectual Property Rights*. (pp. 295-327). The World Bank.

Mathur, S. K. (2003). Trade-related Issues of Intellectual Property Rights and Copyright Provisions: Some Issues with Special Reference to Developing Countries. *The Journal of Intellectual Property Rights , 6* (1), 65-99.

Marx, K. and Engels, F. (1970). Ruling Class and Ruling Ideas. In J. Storey (Ed.). *Cultural Theory and Popular Culture: A Reader* (pp.191-192). Atlanta: University of Georgia Press.

May, C. (2002). Unacceptable Costs: The Consequences of Making Knowledge Property in A Global Society. *Glocal Society , 16* (2). 123-144.

McKormack, G. (1996). *The Spirit of Traditional Chinese Law*. Athens: University of Georgia Press.

Memorandum of Understanding Between the Government of the People's Republic of China and the Government of the United States of America on the Protection of Intellectual Property. (1992). Retrieved August 10, 2009 from Enforcement and Compliance: http://tcc.export.gov/trade_agreements/all_trade_agreements/exp_005362.asp.

Mertha, A. (2005). *The Politics of Piracy: Intellectual Property in Contemporary China*. Ithaca: Cornell University.

Meyer, A. (2001). Technology Transfer Into China: Preparing for A New Era. *European Management*, 19 (2), 140-144.

Morrison, W. M. (2011, January 7). *China - U.S. Trade Issues*. Retrieved May 15, 2011, from Congressional Research Service: http://fpc.state.gov/documents/organization/155009.pdf.

Morrison, W. M. (1995). *The China - U.S. Trade Agreement on Intellectual Property Rights: Implications for China — U.S. Trade Relations*. Congressional Research Service.

National Archives. (n.d.). *Declaration of Indepence: A History*. Retrieved October 1, 2010, from National Archives: http://www.archives.gov/exhibits/charters/declaration_history.html.

Oksenberg, M. P. (1996, Nov). Advancing Intellectual Property Rights: Information Technologies and The Course of Economic Development in China. *NBR Analysis, 7* (4), pp. 1-35.

Oliver, R. (1971). *Communication and Culture In Ancient India and China*. Syracuse: Syracuse Univercity Press.

Parry, B. (2002). Cultures of Knowledge: Investigating Intellectual Property Rights and Relations. *Antipode, 34* (4), 679-706.

Peerenboom, R. (1993). *Asian Discourses of Rule of Law*. Boston: Routledge.

Peerenboom, R. P. (2002). *China's Long March Toward Rule of Law*. Cambridge: Cambridge Univesity Press.

Peerenboom, R. P. (2007). *China Modernizes: Threat to The West or Model for the Rest?* Cambridge: Cambridge University Press.

The Constitution of the People's Republic of China. (2004). Retrieved October 1, 2010, from People's Daily Online: http://english.peopledaily.com.cn/constitution/constitution.html.

Plato. (1996). *Protagoras*. B. Jowett, (Trans.) Amherst: Promethus Books.

Potter, P. B. (2001). *The Chinese Legal System: Globalization and Local legal Culture*. New York: Routledge.

Property Rights Alliance. (2011). *Country Data China*. Retrieved November 5, 2011, from International Property Rights Index 2011 Report: http://www.internationalpropertyrightsindex.org/ATR_2011%20INDEX_Web.pdf.

Ren, X. (1997). *Tradition of the Law and Law of Tradition: Law, State, and Social Control in China*. Westport: Greenwood Press.

Reynolds, N. (1993). Ethos As A Location: New Sites for Discursive Authority. *Rhetoric Review*, 11 (2), 325-338.

Roy, A. (2007). A New Dispute Converning TRIPS Agreement: The United States and China in the WTO. *The Journal of World Intellectual Property*, 476-484.

Samovar, L. A., Porter, R. E., and McDaniel, E. R. (2009). *Communication Between Cultures*. Belmont: Wadsworth Publishing.

Schwabach, A. (2008). Intellectual Property Piracy: Perception and Reality in China, the United States, and Elsewhere. *Journal of International Media and Entertainment Law*, 2 (1), 65-84.

Sell, S. K. (1995). Intellectual Property Protection and Antitrust in the Developing World: Crisis, Coercion, and Choice. *International Organization*, 49 (2), 315-349.

Shi, W. (2006). Cultural Perplexity in Intellectual Property: Is Stealing A Book an Elegant Offense? *North Carolina Journal of International Law & Commercial Regulation*, 32 (1), 1-47.

Storey, J. (2001). *Cultural Theory and Popular Culture*. Boston: Pearson.

---. (1998). *Cultural Theory and Popular Culture: A Reader*. Harlow: Pearson.

Sun Zi. (2005). *The Art of War*. L. Giles (Trans.). El Paso: Norte Press. Retrieved June 10, 2010 from the University of Adelaide Web site: http://ebooks.adelaide.edu.au/s/suntzu/art-of-war/index.html.

Tang, G.H. (2004). A Comparative Study of Copyright and the Public Interest in the United Kingdom and China. 1. *Scripted*. 272-299. DOI: 10.2966/scrip.010204.272.

Thatcher, B. (2001). Adapting to South American Communication Patterns:Odessey's Proposal to Remedy Inconsistent Car Sales. In D. S. Bosley, *Global Contexts: Case Studies in International Technical Communication* (pp. 81-95). Boston: Ally and Bacon.

The Declaration of Independence. Retrieved May 10, 2010 from the Independence Hall Association Web site: http://www.ushistory.org/declaration/document/.

Tully, L. D. (2003). Prospects for Progress: The TRIPS Agreement and Developing Coungtries after the DOHA Conference. *Boston College International and Comparative Law Review*, 26 (1), 129-143.

U. S. Census Bureau. (2011, July). *Top Trading Partners - total Trade, Exports, Imports*. Retrieved September 15, 2011, from Foreign trade: http://www.census.gov/foreign-trade/statistics/highlights/toppartners.html.

USTR. (1995). *The U.S. - China Intellectual Property Rights Agreement: Implications for U.S.-Sino Commercial Relations*. Washington : U.S. Government Printing Office.

---. *The U.S. Special 301 Reports, 1989 to 2011*. Retrieved September 1, 2011, from Knowledge Economy Internationa: Attending and mending the knowledge ecosystem: http://keionline.org/ustr/special301.

Vivian, H. (2005). Copying and Copyright. The Journal of Economic Perspectives, 19 (2), 121-138.

Wang, L. (2004). Intellectual Property Protection in China. *The International Information Library Review*, *36*, 253-261.

WIPO. (2011). *Contracting Parties*. Retrieved June 10, 2011, from WIPO: Encouraging Creativity and Innovation: http://www.wipo.int/treaties/en/ShowResults.jsp?treaty_id=15.

WIPO. (2011). *Summary of the Berne Convention for the Protection of Literary and Artistic Works (1886)*. Retrieved June 10, 2011, from WIPO: Encouraging Creativity and Innovation: http://www.wipo.int/treaties/en/ip/berne/summary_berne.html.

WIPO. (n.d.). *What is Intellectual Property?* Retrieved May 1, 2011, from WIPO: http://www.wipo.int/about-ip/en/.

Xinhua. (2011, August 26). *2007 US v. China Intellectual Property Case*. Retrieved September 1, 2011, from Global Times: http://www.globaltimes.cn/NEWS/tabid/99/ID/672789/2007-US-v-China-Intellectual-Property-Case.aspx.

Yang, D. L. (2003). *Intellectual Property and Doing Business in China*. Bingley: Emerald Group Publishing Limited.

Yu, P. K. (2003). Four Common Misconceptions about Copyright Piracy. *Loyola L. A. Int'l and Comp. L. Rev.*, *26*, pp. 127-150.

Yu, P. K. (2001). From Pirates to Partners: Protecting Intellectual Property in China in the Twenty First Century. *American University Law Review*, *50*, 131-243.

Yu, P. K. (2002). The Second Coming of Intellectual Property Rights in China. *Benjamin N. Cardozo School of Law* (11).

Zheng, Z. Y. and Zong, T. H. (1998). *History of Chinese Rhetoric*. Changchun: Jilin Education Press.